W9-ABY-840

CONSTITUTIONAL RIGHTS AND RELIGIOUS PREJUDICE: CATHOLIC EDUCATION AS THE BATTLEGROUND

CONSTITUTIONAL RIGHTS AND RELIGIOUS PREJUDICE: CATHOLIC EDUCATION AS THE BATTLEGROUND

By Peter M. J. Stravinskas
East Coast Director,
Catholic League for Religious and Civil Rights

Bookmasters Publishing Company

This volume is a revision of a doctoral dissertation
submitted to the School of Education of Fordham
University, under the title of "The Constitutional
Possibilities of Federal Financial Assistance to
Nonpublic School Parents." The mentor was Dr. Thomas
Mulkeen; readers were Dr. Mildred Lee of the School
of Education and the Rev. Charles Whalen, S.J., of
the Law School of Fordham University.

Registration Number: TX 966-558
United States Copyright Office--Library of Congress:
82-13, 623

FOREWORD

This book by Father Peter Stravinskas is a scholarly contribution which is timely and informative.

It is timely because of the urgency of the issue of governmental financial assistance for parents of students in nonpublic schools. If justice is to be served, there must be freedom of choice for these parents in the education of their children. This freedom of choice must not only be theoretical, but also possible for all parents.

It is informative because it examines in an historical and comprehensive manner the important question of the Constitutionality of governmental assistance to nonpublic school parents. The contention of those who oppose such assistance is that it is unconstitutional. All too often, this argumentation is accepted without examination of the information which Father Stravinskas presents.

Legislation can and should be drafted that will not only pass the test of Constitutionality but will enable hundreds of thousands of parents to exercise their constitutional right to freedom of choice in education.

This study will be a help to enable fair-minded persons to examine the issues involved. With many Americans, I look to the day when all parents--of every economic group--will be able to exercise the freedom of choice in the education of their children.

Terence Cardinal Cooke
Archbishop of New York

CONTENTS

CHAPTER I

INTRODUCTION

Controversies frequently arise because of misunderstanding and poor communication. The controversy over government aid to nonpublic school parents is a case in point. The solidifying of positions and the lack of real dialogue have been responsible for more than a century of hard feelings. One of the biggest difficulties has been that the arguments on both sides have been put forth in isolation from the over-arching concerns and broad context. Although the present study has a rather limited scope in terms of its unique contribution to the overall discussion, some preliminary background work was deemed necessary to avoid the pitfalls of duplicating earlier research.

The Present Study: Its Focus

The present study was built on several presuppositions or hypotheses. No researcher is ever totally free of biases. Neutral research, especially in the social sciences and humanities, is not possible and probably not all that desirable. However, it is important for a researcher to expose one's biases to the reader at the outset.

This researcher believes that:

1. Catholic schools are critical to the survival of the Catholic Church in the United States as a distinct entity;

2. While internal ecclesiastical problems certainly bear some responsibility for the decline in American

Catholic education, a major difficulty in the maintenance of the system has been financial;

3. Government assistance, although problematic at both
   the constitutional and policy levels, offers one
   solution that needs further exploration;

4. Respectable constitutional scholars who have opted
   for an alternate reading of the First Amendment's
   strictures have not been adequately heard;

5. Attention must center on the Supreme Court: in its
   interpretation of the First Amendment, in its
   understanding of the nature and purposes of parochial education, in its self-understanding vis a
   vis the legislative branch of government.

The purpose of the study was to discover the constitutional possibilities for federal financial assistance to
nonpublic school parents. Special consideration was given
to the Supreme Court's perception of the nature and purpose
of Catholic schools, as evidenced by dicta in several opinions in which parochial schools are discussed. The research
also sought to determine why the legislative branch of
government has seemed more willing than the judicial to deal
with the question of state aid as a public policy matter
rather than as a hard and fast constitutional issue, and how
the difference in approach has filtered down to the practical level in its effect on nonpublic school parents.

The Study's Significance

The significance of this study is intimately related
to two major areas of concern: fundamental human rights
and the welfare of American education. Since the land-
mark *Pierce* decision [268 U.S. 535 (1925)] of the Supreme
Court, parental freedom of choice in selecting schools for
their children has been taken for granted. Maritain

expressed the principle thus: "The rights of the family,
the rights of the human person as father or mother of the
family, belong to natural law in the strictest sense of the
word."[1]   But this primary parental right appears empty for,
as Blum has argued, "a civil right penalized is a civil
right suppressed."[2]   That is why Hartnett has recalled that
in many nations:

> . . . public support of religious education is
> regarded as necessary in order to protect parents'
> religious freedom and avoid discriminating against
> parents who want to give their children a religious
> education.[3]

Or as Friedman put it, "economic freedom, in and of itself,
is an extremely important part of total freedom."[4]

Furthermore, the survival of parochial education is
essential to the well-being of American education in general.
An alternative school system is most beneficial because by
providing an option, it encourages healthy competition.
Mill spoke out very strongly against a unitary, national
school system:

> That the whole or any or any large part of the
> education of the people be in State hands, I go as
> far as anyone in deprecating. . . . A general state
> education is a mere contrivance for moulding people
> to be exactly like one another.[5]

Denominational education in the United States may well
depend on some renewed appreciation of the critical dimensions of the status quo. Kelly asked a question which is at
the very heart of the present investigations: "Why, in a
word, should old arguments, old fears, old prejudices,
interfere with a relevant view of a very new problem--the
very existence of private lower education?"[6]

This study is meaningful because it deals with basic
rights guaranteed by the Constitution and because it further
concerns itself with a matter related to the totality of

American education, in which religiously-oriented schools
play a special and significant role.

This particular study is likewise relevant to the needs
of parochial school administrators and all concerned with
the questions raised and the data uncovered by the research
project. A personal letter from the Rev. Msgr. John F.
Meyers, President of the National Catholic Educational
Association, added further support to this belief:

> As I already expressed personally to you, I
> think your topic is a good one, and an important
> one. The main obstacle to government support of
> private schools has been the U.S. Supreme Court.
> The evidence in their decisions seems to show an
> abysmal ignorance of what goes on in a Catholic
> school. This is, of course, my hypothesis. Only a
> study such as you contemplate would test it.
>   It would seem that anything we can do to give
> both the court and the general public an awareness
> of the facts would be most helpful in our federal
> aid campaigns. If the justices have the wrong
> impression of Catholic schools, we should get the
> facts and call their error to their attention.[7]

This work represents an attempt at synthesis, analysis
and dissemination of the data.

The Uniqueness of the Study

The present study is unique in that it proceeds along
the lines of a multi-disciplinary analysis of a question
which heretofore has been limited to legal or historical
research. To the legal and historical dimensions are added
the theological, sociological and philosophical. This has
the effect of broadening the context and opening the discussion up to the insights of these other disciplines.

Its uniqueness is especially evident in two areas of
investigation which have not benefited from research to
date. Although the Supreme Court in both *Everson* and
Lemon has said that the image or profile of the parochial

school is a determining factor in granting or not granting government aid, no research has been done to discover what the composite picture is in the mind of the Court, how related it really is to aid decisions, and from what sources the Court's profile comes.

Yet another unique contribution is an examination of the parochial school aid controversy as a confrontation between the legislative and judicial branches of government rather than simply a Church-State conflict.

The Methodology of the Study

The methodology employed in the study combines descriptive and inferential lines of analysis. Both primary and secondary sources were used. Public documents like state legal codes, Supreme Court opinions, the Congressional Record, and briefs filed in the cases involving governmental assistance to nonpublic school parents formed the backbone of the research material. These were augmented by personal interviews with key people connected with the topic; the research was rounded out by reference to noted commentators, especially in the fields of history and jurisprudence.

The heart of the discussion begins with a chapter on the theological and sociological rationale for education in a value-oriented, religious environment. Successive chapters deal with the public policy question of federal assistance to nonpublic school parents, followed by the constitutional question. The remaining chapters explore how the legislatures have demonstrated a willingness to aid parental freedom of choice, how the Supreme Court has responded to those attempts, what the Court has said about parochial schools, and how valid those observations have been.

The study ends with conclusions and recommendations.

NOTES

CHAPTER I

[1]Jacques Maritain, *The Rights of Man and Natural Law* (New York: Scribner's, 1947), p. 82.

[2]Virgil Blum, *Freedom in Education* (Garden City, N.Y.: Doubleday, 1965), p. 56.

[3]Robert Hartnett, ed., *The Right to Educate* (New York: America Press, 1949), p. 4.

[4]Milton Friedman, *Capitalism and Freedom* (Chicago: University of Chicago Press, 1972), p. 9.

[5]John Stuart Mill, *On Liberty* (New York: Henry Holt & Co., 1898), p. 188.

[6]George Kelly, ed., *Government Aid to Nonpublic Schools: Yes or No?* (New York: St. John's University Press, 1972), p. 60.

[7]John Meyers, personal letter, 20 December 1979.

CHAPTER II

GOALS AND DIFFICULTIES IN CATHOLIC EDUCATION

Theological Reflections on Catholic Education

The purpose of this chapter is to familiarize the reader with theological and sociological considerations on providing a total education in a value-oriented environment. An overview of the birth, growth and problems of Catholic education in the country situates the present question in an historical light.

The Dogmatic Constitution on the Church *(Lumen Gentium)* of Vatican II launched the Church on a new path toward self-evaluation and self-realization. This document preferred to use the image "People of God" to describe the Church, stressing the communitarian nature of the Church's life, and "Pilgrim People", signifying a community in the process of becoming more than it is, and en route to its final goal. In the wake of this renewed awareness of its existence came additional insights, not the least of which was the designation of the family as "the domestic Church."[1]

This development tended to place the ultimate responsibility for the education of children on parents,[2] not on the institutional Church, as had so often been the case before. In reality, the Church has always taught that parents are the primary educators of their children;[3] practice, however, often overclouded theory. While holding to this critical principle of theology (and sociology), it would be foolish to assume that "primary" would mean "only". Some parents took their new-found dignity and responsibility

so seriously that they attempted to perform the task of edu-
cating their children in moral values independently of the
institutional Church. One would have to admit that many
laity received more than a little encouragement along those
lines from clergy and religious educators who had grossly
misread and misinterpreted some of the Second Vatican
Council's documents and had completely overlooked still
others.

Some opinion-makers in the Church raised questions about
the institutional Church's commitment to and understanding
of Catholic education as it had been traditionally understood since the Catholic school curriculum had become similar in many ways to that of the public schools. Regular
school closings, an increased reliance on lay teachers, and
a new stress on out-of-school religious education programs
as viable alternatives were also operative factors. Another
concern raised at the time was whether or not parochial
schools fostered a ghetto mentality, causing Catholics to be
unassimilated into the mainstream of American life. Add to
all this a decline in Catholic births, similar to that of
the overall American population. The end result found dra-
matic expression in the thousands of Catholic parents who
withdrew their children from Catholic schools, or never
enrolled them at all either because they did not have any or
because parental confidence in the schools (and the Church)
had been shaken.

Fifteen years later, and much wiser for the experience,
the Catholic community has demonstrated a renewed interest
in Catholic education as enrollments have stabilized and
even increased in many dioceses.[4] Some of this change of
heart has come about because parents realize they need positive reinforcement of their values in the classroom; the
secular humanism of the public schools cannot help them in

that area and, in some cases, actively opposes their value system, to the confusion of the children.

A deeper appreciation of the Church as a community has also fixed the idea firmly that there exists a diversity of gifts and ministries.[5] The role of parents is to plant the seed of faith and to nurture its growth. Usually, however, they will need the assistance of professional educators to see that the seed blossoms.

This consciousness has guided the Church's understanding of the educational process from the very beginning and goes a long way to explain its intense commitment to providing a total education in a value-oriented atmosphere. There has been an amazing consistency on this, as even a brief survey of ecclesiastical documents would reveal. The present study deals with those which have had an impact on the Church in the United States.

The First Provincial Council of Baltimore in 1829 asserted that "we judge it absolutely necessary that schools be established in which the young may be taught the principles of faith and morality, while being instructed in letters."[6] The bishops of the nation made their judgment a matter of law in 1884 at the Third Plenary Council of Baltimore: "We decide and decree that near each church, where it does not exist, a parish school is to be erected within two years from the promulgation of this Council."[7] Between those two Councils had come the Irish immigration, with its unique problems. Undoubtedly, the American bishops saw new urgency to give concrete form to their earlier vision.

Some American bishops, like John Ireland, opted for an approach to Catholicism that one might anachronistically dub "assimilationism". The Americanist point of view maintained that Catholic doctrine should be presented in a way that would cause as little difference to surface with Protestants as possible. Educationally, the Americanists were opposed to parochial schools. The "Americanist heresy" was finally responded to--and negatively--by Pope Leo XIII in his 1899 letter to Cardinal Gibbons, *Testem Benevolentiae.*

The Code of Canon Law, enacted in 1918 for the universal Church, has this strong statement: "Catholic children are not to attend non-Catholic, neutral or mixed schools."[8] Where no other alternative was possible, the bishop himself had to determine what dangers to the faith existed and then judge if a dispensation from the law would be tolerable. The rationale behind this stringent injunction was explained clearly by Pope Pius XI in his encyclical "On the Christian Education of Youth":

> . . . the so-called 'neutral' school from which religion is excluded, is contrary to the fundamental principles of education. Such a school moreover cannot exist in practice; it is bound to become irreligious.[9]

While this kind of thinking has been characterized as a "fortress" or "siege mentality", few observers can doubt that the American public school is a clear example of a "neutral" school system becoming "irreligious" *de facto* and, some would add, *de jure.*

The Fathers of the Second Vatican Council dealt with Catholic education extensively as they followed the trajectory of Church teaching to that point and contributed to its development as well. Several comments bear notice from their Declaration on Christian Education:

> The Church's involvement in the field of education is demonstrated especially by the Catholic school. . . . Therefore, since it can contribute so substantially to fulfilling the mission of God's people, and can further the dialogue between the Church and the family of man, to their mutual bene-

fit, the Catholic school retains its immense importance in the circumstances of our times too. . . .
    As for Catholic parents, the Council calls to
mind their duty to entrust their children to
Catholic schools. . . .[10]

In 1971 the American bishops issued a pastoral letter on
Catholic education, "To Teach as Jesus Did." It became the
standard by which to judge all Catholic schools, outlining
as it did the goals and objectives for all Catholic institutions of learning. Included is the following statement:
"[They] are the most effective means available to the Church
for the education of children and young people."[11] Many
would point to the great irony that at the very moment of
this letter's promulgation, pastors were closing schools at
an unprecedented rate, usually with the blessing of the
local bishop.

Pope Paul VI's bicentennial message to the Church in the
United States contained praise for the American Catholic
school system and an encouragement to continue the tradition:
"The strength of the Church in America [is] in the Catholic
schools."[12] Nor was it sheer coincidence that the two
Americans Paul VI canonized in observance of our bicentennial, Bishop John Neumann of Philadelphia[13] and Mother
Elizabeth Seton of New York,[14] were prime movers in the
parochial school effort.

The most thorough analysis of Catholic education in
modern times was offered by the Vatican's Sacred Congregation
for Catholic Education in 1977. "The Catholic School"
probed every aspect of the educational process and also
recognized the fact that some people had suggested the
phasing out of Catholic schools. Its conclusion was that
"to give in to them would be suicidal."[15]

Pope John Paul II's esteem for the American Catholic
school system has been demonstrated on several occasions.

Just months after his installation, he sent a videotaped message to Catholic educators gathered in Philadelphia for the annual convention of the National Catholic Educational Association, in which he said that he hoped to give "a new impulse to Catholic education throughout the vast area of the United States of America." He went on to say: "Yes, the Catholic school must remain *a privileged means of Catholic education in America.*"[16] Later that year during his pastoral visit to the United States, with 20,000 Catholic school students at Madison Square Garden, he seized the opportunity "to tell [them] why the Church considers it so important and expends so much energy in order to provide . . . millions of young people with a Catholic education."[17] He has likewise referred to the Catholic school as "the heart of the Church."[18]

The doctrinal commitment to the maintenance of the parochial school system in the United States, then, can be seen to be strong, impressive and consistent. That is, the statements of those at the highest levels of the hierarchy have been strong, impressive and consistent. Once again, however, the living out of the verbal commitment has sometimes been found wanting, especially in recent years.

If it is true that the Church is essentially a gathering of people, a sociology of religion in general and religious education in particular would not be out of order. Sociologists have had much to say on both topics, and their insights are most germane to the present study, especially since so much of the theological commitment to Catholic education has strong sociological underpinnings.

Sociological Reflections on Religiously-Oriented
Educational Institutions

The United States has traditionally prided itself on
being a pluralistic society. The very expression, however,
is fraught with problems because divergent interpretations
of pluralism are possible, as Greeley has noted: "The two
principal models for viewing the phenomenon of ethnicity and
acculturation in the United States are the melting pot model
of the assimilationists and the mosaic model of the cultural
pluralists."[19] Since American society has become more sensitized to minorities and the importance of maintaining con-
tinuity with one's cultural and ethnic roots, the melting
pot theory has fallen into disfavor since it "usually means
Anglo conformity."[20] The mosaic model, then, would seem to
be viable since it enables diversity to flourish within a
unity of purpose, achieving unity without uniformity.

The American public school, born of the religious conflicts and compromises of the 19th Century, was charged with
serving as "the nation's main agency of assimilation and
Americanization."[21] Lynn's observations shed much light on
where parochial schools fitted, or did not fit, into the
whole process. According to him, the controversy over
government aid to such institutions was frequently rooted in
anti-Catholic prejudice but, even more importantly, due to
"some deeply held convictions about the nature of the
[American] public."[22] He went on to explain the nature of
those convictions:

> In 'the nation with the soul of a church' the
> public school had taken on a sacral character. And
> thus the defense of public education became an
> exercise in political ecclesiology. This interpre-
> tation helps to explain the devout tone so evident
> in their protective praising of the public school,
> and the absoluteness with which they rejected any
> hint of state grants for parochial schools. By its

very nature as a 'sectarian' institution, the
Catholic school was ill-equipped to pass on the
public faith, fully and freely expressed, to the
coming generation.[23]

The key questions that emerge are two: As a nation, do
we support (in reality, not in theory) the socialization of
the melting pot (assimilation) or of the mosaic (pluralism)?
As a nation, do we believe alternatives to government
schools can adequately accomplish the State's legitimate
interests? The Dutch have answered both questions in the
affirmative, and their public policy and practice demonstrate
this clearly:

> The Dutch system of putting public and private
> education on an equal footing in both a formal and
> a material sense is unique, and is to be found in
> no other country in the world to the same extent.
> The Dutch public regards it as a prized possession,
> because it enables every section of the population
> to give expression in its own way to the spiritual
> values that it considers of fundamental importance
> and to make its own contribution to the development
> of the community.[24]

The witness of dozens of nations that financially support complete parental freedom of choice in education,
as well as pluralism, and the attractiveness of genuine
competition among educational institutions have caused
educators like Sizer to conclude that "as a matter or
public policy, education should move toward institutional
pluralism."[25] This opinion would obviously hold that a
multiplicity of educational forms would more accurately
reflect the multiplicity of publics forming the American
nation, leading to an enhancement of the overall educational
process and final output. Butts would certainly disagree
with such a philosophy and policy since he understands
governmental goals in education thus:

The prime purpose for a public rather than a
private education was *political;* it was to prepare
the young for their role as self-governing citizens
rather than as subjects bound to an alien sovereign
or as *private persons* loyal to their families,
their kinsfolk, their churches, their localities or
neighborhoods, or their ethnic traditions. In its
origin, the idea of public education was *not* to
promote the individual needs and interests of
children, *not* to prepare for a better job, *not* to
get into college.[26]

For a religious body to operate schools, assurance is
needed that the effort and expenditure in some way achieve
commensurate results. The only serious research on Catholic
education in the United States has been done by Greeley; his
conclusions in 1977 and 1981 indicated that Catholic schools
are needed now more than ever for the American Catholic community, and that these schools are, in fact, producing the
desired effects.[27]

A nation, on the other hand, can intelligently permit
only those educational institutions to exist that fulfill
its goals of providing the necessary academic information
and of fostering good citizenship. Moynihan noted that the
crux of the problem lies in that second area of concern:

This has not been a matter of educational
quality, still less of efficiency. In the main,
the nonpublic schools are just as good and, in the
main, startlingly cheaper. It has been a matter of
ideology; of legitimacy. It was not enough to say
that public schools provide the basic educational
resource of the republic. . . . It became necessary
to stigmatize the other schools as 'foreign' or
'elitist', or threatening. The new schools became
clothed with a public purpose that increasingly was
denied the older schools.[28]

Greeley's research has indicated that:

There is no evidence of Catholic schools being
divisive. On the contrary, those who attend them
seem to be more supportive of racial integration

and have a higher level of 'social consciousness' than those who do not attend Catholic schools.[29]

If the government had substantial doubts about the socialization process that occurs in denominational schools, the logical move would be to close such institutions. This was the obvious intent of the statute enacted in Oregon in the second decade of this century when nonpublic schools were outlawed. The Supreme Court, however, in its *Pierce* decision of 1925 declared such a law to be beyond legitimate state interest and a violation of parental rights in directing the education of their children.[30] For all its obvious failings, the Oregon statute had this much to recommend it: Convinced that alternate educational institutions were bad, they were closed--rather than simply being made difficult to attend. Such thinking, though, is not completely a matter of history. Butts has, without going to the extreme of the Oregon statute, come very close to that position by arguing that "the common foundation of civic learning is all the more reason for the children and youth not to be separated into special ability tracks or into separate private, parochial, or public schools."[31]

However, it is too late in the day of American national life to revert to that pre-Pierce position because parental rights are clearly established by law. Society has become too sensitized to its racial and ethnic richness to suggest officially a return to the predominant WASP culture of pre-immigration days. The value of a total education in a religious ambience is too well appreciated by ever-increasing numbers of people within our society for the religious communities themselves to decide to abandon the educational enterprise for, as Neusner asked, "without institutions and organizations to give direction and substance to the life of such groups, what is left but inchoate sentiment?[32] Surely this is what was meant by the assertion that Hebrew Day schools are necessary for "a truly meaningful Jewish community in America."[33]

The theology and sociology of religiously-sponsored secular education leads logically to *"the policy field,* heavily surcharged with considerations of public welfare in a pluralistic society with a democratic base."[34] Doyle argued that:

> As the middle class goes so goes public policy. It should be no surprise, then, that private schools are beginning to move closer to the top of the nation's education agenda. Equally, it should be no surprise that the principal public policy question is whether or not private schools should receive public funds.[35]

Even Butts had admitted that: "Pluralism has had a rapid rise in popularity among an increasing number of critics of public education during the past decade or so."[36]

Sizer mused on where educational pluralism might lead. He saw Roman Catholics in the forefront of the movement to give institutional expression to the principle of educational pluralism. His conclusion was a cautious prognostication based on socio-political realities: "In fact, this day may represent the darkness before the dawn for them; they may be the harbingers of a pattern politically acceptable in the late seventies and 1980's."[37]

This study was designed to investigate some of the socio-political realities that might well clarify the state of the question in such a way that a "politically acceptable" pattern can be discovered which will serve both Church and State, thus resolving a century-long conflict which has helped no one and has often seriously hampered the achievement of quality education in both public and private schools.

Important Moments in the History of American
Catholic Education

The first school within the territorial expanse of what
is now the United States was a Catholic school, established
by the Franciscans in Florida in 1606.[38] The opening of
schools in all the Spanish territories was a pattern
followed in California and New Mexico as the Franciscans
sought to educate the children of both the colonists and the
native Americans.

The French exploration of the New World led to the
opening of the first school for boys in New Orleans in 1722
by a Capuchin friar; the Ursuline nuns began a girls' school
in that city five years later.[39] These schools became pro-
totypes of those to spring up along the St. Lawrence River
and in St. Louis, Kaskaskia, Mackinaw, Detroit, Vincennes
and Maine (where a Catholic school existed as early as
1640).[40]

In the British colonies Catholics experienced relative
freedom only in Maryland, as long as Catholics ruled, and in
Pennsylvania; it was in places such as these that Catholic
education began its development into the system it is today.
The groundwork laid during the colonial period served as the
foundation for the massive Catholic educational effort that
would flourish within fifty years of the ratification of the
Constitution.

Much of what parochial schools became and still are came
about through a series of events played out in New York
City. The chief protagonist (or antagonist, as some would
see it) was Archbishop John Hughes who, from 1840 to 1842,
was embroiled in a heated controversy over Catholic children
and their education. His first complaint centered on the
overt anti-Catholicism in the so-called public schools.
When assurances were given that the most offensive aspects

of this bigotry would be stopped, he next attacked Bible-reading in the schools as a sectarian religious exercise, unacceptable to the Catholic community. He was joined in this battle by Unitarians, Jews, other religious minorities, and atheists. Unwittingly, he may well have paved the way for the secular humanism which now prevails in America's public schools.[41]

His most notable achievement was gaining for the immigrants the right to operate and control their own schools. He was unsuccessful in obtaining public funds for the schools, however, and began to rely on religious orders to provide low-cost, quality education, moving away from the lay teachers who actually predominated in the Catholic schools before that time. His decision to abandon the battle with secular authorities served as further impetus for the establishment of a separate school system for American Catholics. He believed strongly and sincerely that "the days have come, and the place, in which the school is more necessary than the church."[42] Shaw has suggested that Hughes felt that if he lost the children, there would be little hope for the future of American Catholicism.[43]

Not all American bishops agreed with Hughes on either the necessity of Catholic schools or the desirability of state aid. Archbishop John Ireland of St. Paul uttered cautious but clear statements of his desire to utilize the public schools. The "Poughkeepsie Plan" was a compromise effort to have Catholic children partially under ecclesiastical jurisdiction and partially under state control. His suggestions along these lines were vehemently attacked by many of his brother-bishops, most notably, by John Lancaster Spaulding, Bishop of Peoria. He contended, like Hughes, that "without parish schools, there is no hope that the Church will be able to maintain itself in

America."[44]   Unlike Hughes, though, Spaulding recoiled from
the thought of any kind of governmental assistance for
parochial schools.

While the first Catholic school operated on this con-
tinent as early as 1606, it took over two centuries for
these institutions to be organized into anything resembling
a system.   A German-born Redemptorist and naturalized
American citizen named John Neumann accomplished that feat.
As the third bishop of Philadelphia, Neumann established a
Diocesan Board of Education with clerical and lay representatives from every parish in the Diocese.   Through this body
of advisors and due to his own personal drive, parochial
education prospered in Philadelphia and became a unified,
coherent system, making Philadelphia a model for the nation
and Neumann "the father of parochial schools in America."[45]

By 1892, Archbishop Patrick John Ryan had appointed a
Philadelphia priest to full-time work as diocesan superintendent of schools.   The commitment to Catholic education
continued to grow and under Cardinal Dennis Dougherty
(1918-1951), a unique system of free Catholic high schools
flourished.   What was a priority for the Ordinary was
expected to be a priority for his clergy, as pastors unwill-
ing to open parish schools were threatened with removal.[46]

The strong organizational beginnings in New York and
Philadelphia spread throughout the country, so that American
Catholics could boast of the largest privately-sponsored
school system in the world by the 1950's and the 1960's.
Then the bottom seemed to fall out.

Financial Problems and Government Aid

The Catholic school decline between 1965 and 1975 was
precipitous; approximately a school a day closed its doors
at the beginning of that period, finally resulting in an

enrollment decline of 36% from the peak year of 1964.[47]
While a single-cause theory of events is naive, that finances
were a major problem cannot be denied. This finding was
ultimately incorporated into a report of President Nixon's
Committee on Nonpublic Education.[48] In days of high inflation, attention is logically turned away from already over-
burdened parochial school parents to the government at its
various levels.

The suggestion to look to the government for help 20
years ago (and it was discussed then) would have experienced
a doubtful and even hostile reception in the general population. That is no longer the case. Testimony to the new
attitude comes from several public opinion polls.

In 1970 the Gallup Poll asked, "Do you favor or oppose
giving some government tax money to help parochial schools?"
Forty-eight percent said they favored aid; 44% did not.[49]
A 1974 Gallup Poll sought public attitudes regarding a
possible constitutional amendment to permit aid to parochial
schools. Fifty-two percent of the population sampled favored
such a change, with 35% opposed and 13% undecided.[50] A 1979
New York Times-CBS Poll discovered that 60% of those surveyed "favored income tax advantages to help pay for tuition
at private and parochial schools; 35% did not."[51]

The responses given in the three polls demonstrate a
progressively more favorable public climate and are a far
cry from the sentiments which led to convent-burnings and
the introduction of Blaine Amendments (enacted to forbid
state aid to parochial schools) into state constitutions
during the last century. This development could be attrib-
uted to a good public relations job done by the parochial
school community in recent years; it could be but one more
indicator of the general dissatisfaction with public education; it might be the result of a more liberal, educated

society in which many former fears of aid to religious
schools were the remnants of latent but long-standing anti-
Catholicism.

Hitchcock has argued that the political coming of age of
American Catholics that was achieved with Kennedy's election
as President (after his willingness to suffer public humil-
iation by Protestant clergy in Houston) and the calling
of the Second Vatican Council occurred only because the
Catholic Church was no longer perceived as a threat. He
explains that:

> [W]hile the Council was being officially and
> publicly proclaimed a triumph, the real message
> that was being beamed to the public was that it was
> a surrender, voluntary and unexpected, with scarce-
> ly any advance warnings or signs of weakness in the
> institution. It was not only a surrender in the
> sense of the abandonment of long-held beliefs and
> practices but also a surrender, or a relaxation, on
> a personal level. . . . The image of the Church as
> a loser, a declining institution admitting that it
> had taught and practiced error for centuries, came
> to dominate the imaginations of many people includ-
> ing many Catholics, often subconsciously.[52]

Whatever the correct explanation or explanations, the data
suggest a decided change in thinking.

In the face of a financial crisis, it is not strange
that those concerned with the continued existence of a
parochial school system in the United States should begin to
search for additional sources of revenue. One possibility
is governmental assistance, justified on the grounds that
parochial schools serve a public function. Chief Justice
Warren Burger, in his dissent in *Committee for Public Education and Religious Liberty v. Nyquist,* acknowledged the need
for state aid in 1973, when he observed:

> I would therefore uphold these New York and
> Pennsylvania statutes. However sincere our collec-
> tive protestations of the debt owed by the public

generally to the parochial school system, the wholesome diversity they engender will not survive on
expression of good will.[53]

If parochial schools need funds so badly, one could ask
why the government does not then provide assistance, as it
has in so many other situations. The answer is to be found
in modern interpretations of 16 words of the First Amendment
to the Constitution of the United States: "Congress shall
make no law respecting an establishment of religion, or prohibiting the free exercise thereof . . ."[54] After nearly
150 years of that Amendment's life, it came to mean, among
other things, that the most significant types of financial
aid to denominational schools are forbidden.

From the *Everson* bus case of 1947 to the present, the
Supreme Court of the United States has handled dozens of
cases involving Church-State relations, including the specific issue of aid to parochial schools. While the justices
in the preponderance of cases have interpreted the First
Amendment as restrictive of general aid to religious schools,
important concessions have been made. Even if all the decisions were negative, discussion and study would still be in
order since, as Corwin said:

> . . . judicial review *considered as a method
> for interpreting the Constitution is an inter-
> mediate not a final process.* For while judicial
> construction of the Constitution is final for the
> case in which it is pronounced, it is not final
> against the political forces to which a changed
> opinion may give rise, whether in the legislature,
> or in the judiciary itself. Furthermore, it is
> legitimate--indeed to be expected--that public
> opinion will be agitated to bring about just such
> changes in it.[55]

One might be tempted to accept the Supreme Court's decisions as infallible and irreformable. They are not, asserted
Moynihan. He would further maintain that the Court can err,

and has indeed erred in the past. When confronted with judicial error, Moynihan suggested the following steps to effect a correction: debate, litigate, legislate.[56] The present research is, in part, a step toward greater clarification of the issue at hand.

In reacting to these Supreme Court decisions, a number of points need to be considered. First of all, the Court has not taken a clear, unequivocal stand on this issue to date. This fact caused Byrnes to declare: "It seems that one of the keys to unlocking some of the doors to clarity would be to have some concise Supreme Court decisions that guide rather than confuse."[57]

A second consideration has been raised by Corwin in his role as a constitutional scholar: "In short, while the Court can and must decide *cases* according to its own independent view of the Constitution, it does not in so doing decide questions."[58] His corollary is also important because of its implications for the political process in terms of the on-going move toward a liberalized policy of granting government aid to religious schools: "It [the Court] does not . . . fix the *Constitution* for an indefinite future."[59] In other words, the Court does not have the power to decide on this matter, or any other, in a once-and-for-all manner; it can only react to various aid programs that come before it for review and pass on their constitutionality, and not on the universal question.

Third, a context for these cases would provide the possibility of perspective. That an inconsistent yardstick has been employed by the Court in this area has been alleged by many. Corwin put it thus: "The Court seems to cherish a strange tenderness for outre religious manifestations which contrasts sharply with its attitude toward organized religion."[60] Sorauf went so far as to say:

> The school cases, it is no exaggeration to say,
> constitute the most important subset of Church-
> State cases. . . . They also alarm all separation-
> ists and public education interests who see any
> alliance between religion and public schools, and
> between public treasuries and religious schools, as
> a threat to the ideal of the secular, pluralistic
> public school.[61]

The crux of the problem, and its resolution, may lie in this sphere of the apparent, or at least seeming, dichotomy of approach of the Court in Church-State cases.

A fourth line of investigation lay in the necessity of giving due cognizance to factors beyond the constitutional question as exerting an influence in the formation of Supreme Court decisions. Sorauf's study "suggests, as well, something of the community context and group conflict in which the litigation develops, and of the broader policy problems and social attitudes behind it."[62]

Fifth, it is important to note that state legislators and even federal congressmen have demonstrated a willingness to adopt a more pragmatic approach in the parochial school aid controversy, believing that limited aid could forestall a mass exodus into public schools. Surely it is no accident that if the push for governmental assistance can be geo-graphically determined by the states of origin for Supreme Court litigation on this topic (New Jersey, New York, Pennsylvania, Rhode Island, Ohio), then one would not be incorrect in concluding that they happen to coincide with areas of high parochial school enrollment and high Catholic population. The courts, especially the Supreme Court, have tended to disagree with the respective legislatures on such a pragmatic approach, leading Tortora to remark that this is merely one more example of "another of the usurpations that bestrew the path of the Court."[63]

Sixth, another concern must be that, assuming aid to parochial schools is deemed constitutional, is it desirable? Is it desirable for the parochial schools, which may have to accept certain governmental regulations and restrictions? Is it desirable for the public schools which could be left with only those incorrigible or unteachable students not wanted in private schools?

Finally, several judicial statements have signaled that the Supreme Court is as concerned with the profile of the parochial school, that is, those elements that comprise its character, identity or image, as much as it is concerned with the First Amendment itself. This came out clearly in *Lemon v. Kurtzman:*

> In order to determine whether the government entanglement with religion is excessive, we must examine the character and purposes of the institutions that are benefited, the nature of the aid that the State provides, and the resulting relationship between the government and the religious authority.[64]

Many observers have noted a definite correlation between the Catholicity of parochial schools and the resultant prohibitions of state aid. Katz's reading of history brought him to conclude that this posture has been "associated with successive waves of anti-Catholic feeling."[65] Sorauf spelled this out in greater detail:

> Politically, educationally, and constitutionally, the most important fact about alternatives to public education in the United States is that they are largely Roman Catholic. . . . It is not much of an exaggeration to say that the debate over public support for private education in the United States is in fact debate over aid to Catholic schools.[66]

The present study, then, was multi-dimensional in scope for, as Yudof said:

Studies limited to Supreme Court decisions fail
to capture the richness of the legal environment in
which school professionals operate.

Furthermore, the focus on reform and the
Constitution had led many lawyer-researchers to
ignore the wisdom of other disciplines except in
the most superficial adversary ways. . . .[67]

This research was also based on Yudof's belief that
"education is too important to be left to educators, and
law-and-education research is too important to be left to
lawyers,"[68] especially since "lawyers frequently do not know
much about how schools operate, and they often do not wish
to learn."[69]

NOTES

CHAPTER II

[1]Walter Abbott and Joseph Gallagher, eds., *The Documents of Vatican II* (New York: Guild Press, 1966), p. 29.

[2]*Ibid.,* p. 641.

[3]cf. Pope Pius XI, *Christian Education of Youth* (Washington: National Catholic Welfare Conference, 1936).

[4]See: "Diocese Schools Show Increased Enrollments," *The [Trenton] Monitor,* 3 November 1980, p. 18.

[5]See: Abbott and Gallagher, pp. 56-65 *(supra,* note 1).

[6]Peter Guilday, *A History of the Councils of Baltimore* (New York: Arno Press & NYT, 1969), p. 94.

[7]*Decreta Concilii Baltimorensis Tertii* (Baltimore: John Murphy and Company, 1886), p. 104.

[8]Pope Pius X, *Codex Iuris Canonici* (Westminster, Md.: Newman Press, 1963), Canon 1374, p. 471.

[9]Pius XI, p. 30 *(supra,* note 3).

[10]Abbott and Gallagher, p. 647 *(supra,* note 1).

[11]National Conference of Catholic Bishops, *To Teach as Jesus Did* (Washington: United States Catholic Conference, 1972), p. 33.

[12]Pope Paul VI, "Heritage of Freedom," *The Pope Speaks* 21 (1976): 241.

[13]Paul VI, "A Life of Love for Others," *The Pope Speaks* 22 (1977): 223.

[14]Paul VI, "Elizabeth Ann Seton," *The Pope Speaks* 20 (1975): 207.

[15]Sacred Congregation for Catholic Education, *The Catholic School* (Washington: United States Catholic Conference, 1977), p. 64.

[16]Pope John Paul II, "Pope's Message on Catholic Education," *l'Osservatore Romano,* 30 April 1979, p. 4.

[17]John Paul II, "The Church Wants to Communicate Christ to You," *USA: The Message of Justice, Peace and Love* (Boston: St. Paul Editions, 1979), p. 90.

[18]"Pope: Schools Are Heart of Church," *Catholic Standard and Times,* 26 November 1981, p. 12.

[19]Andrew Greeley, *The American Catholic* (New York: Basic Books, 1977), p. 28.

[20]*Ibid.,* p. 23.

[21]Edwin Gaustad, *A Religious History of America* (New York: Harper and Row, 1974), p. 213.

[22]Robert Lynn, "The Eclipse of a Public," *Theology and Church in Times of Change* (Philadelphia: Westminster Press, 1970), p. 199.

[23]*Ibid.*

[24]"Education and Science," *The Kingdom of the Netherlands* (The Hague: Government Printing Office, 1971), p. 9.

[25]Theodore Sizer, "Education and Assimilation," *Phi Delta Kappan* 58 (September 1976): 35.

[26]R. Freeman Butts, "Education Vouchers," *Phi Delta Kappan* 61 (September 1979): 7.

[27]See: Andrew Greeley, *Catholic Schools in a Declining Church* (Kansas City: Sheed and Ward, 1976) and *Young Catholics in the United States and Canada* (New York: Sadlier & Co., 1981).

[28]Daniel Moynihan, "Why Private Schools Merit Public Aid," *Independent School* 37 (May 1978): 18.

[29]Andrew Greeley, *An Ugly Little Secret* (Kansas City: Andrews and McMeel, 1977), p. 185.

[30]See: *Pierce v. Society of Sisters,* 268 U.S. 535 (1925).

[31]R. Freeman Butts, *The Revival of Civic Learning* (Bloomington, Ind.: Phi Delta Kappa Educational Foundation, 1980), p. 131.

[32]Jacob Neusner, "How Should Jews Vote?" *National Review* 32 (17 October 1980): 1252.

[33]Adon Taft, "Day Schools Are Key to Survival, Rabbi Says," *Miami Herald*, 3 April 1981, p. E5.

[34]Henry Abraham, *Freedom and the Court* (New York: Oxford University Press, 1976), p. 276.

[35]Denis Doyle, "Public Policy and Private Education," *Phi Delta Kappan* 62 (September 1980):   17.

[36]Butts, p. 10 *(supra, note 31)*.

[37]Sizer, p. 35 *(supra, note 25)*.

[38]James Burns, et al., *A History of Catholic Education in the United States* (New York: Benziger Bros., 1937), p. 35.

[39]*Ibid.*, p. 29.

[40]*Ibid.*, p. 35.

[41]See: Richard Shaw, *Dagger John: The Life of Archbishop John Hughes* (New York: Paulist Press, 1977).

[42]Burns, p. 160 *(supra, note 38)*.

[43]Shaw, p. 224 *(supra, note 41)*.

[44]Davis Sweeney, *The Life of John Lancaster Spaulding* (New York: Herder and Herder, 1966), p. 216.

[45]Sacred Congregation for the Causes of Saints, *Decree of Canonization of John Nepomucene Neumann* (Rome, 13 November 1976).

[46]James Connelly, ed., *The History of the Archdiocese of Philadelphia* (Philadelphia: Archdiocese of Philadelphia, 1976), p. 354.

[47]Daniel Sullivan, *Public Aid to Nonpublic Schools* (Lexington, Mass.: Heath and Co., 1974), p. 25.

[48]See: President's Panel on Nonpublic Education, *Nonpublic Education and the Common Good* (Washington: U.S. Government Printing Office, 1972).

[49]Stanley Elam, ed., *A Decade of Gallup Polls of Attitudes Toward Education* (Bloomington, Ind.:   Phi Delta Kappa, 1978), p. 60.

[50]*Ibid.*, p. 197.

[51]Adam Clymer, "Carter Budget Gets Support in Survey," *New York Times,* 31 January 1979, p. 1+.

[52]James Hitchcock, *On the Present Position of Catholics in America* (New York: National Committee of Catholic Laymen, 1978), pp. 9-10.

[53]413 U.S. 823 (1973).

[54]Thomas Lawler, *Standard History of America* (New York: Ginn and Co., 1937), p. xxxi.

[55]Edward Corwin, *Court over Constitution* (Gloucester, Mass.:   Peter Smith Publishers, 1957), p. 61.

[56]See: Daniel Moynihan, "What Do You Do When the Supreme Court Is Wrong?" *The Public Interest* 57 (Fall 1979):   3-24.

[57]Lawrence Byrnes, *Religion and Public Education* (New York: Harper and Row, 1975), p. 120.

[58]Edward Corwin, *American Constitutional History* (New York: Harper Torchbooks, 1964), p. 131.

[59]Corwin, p. 74 *(supra,* note 55).

[60]Corwin, *A Constitution of Powers in a Secular State* (Charlottesville, Va.:   Michie Co., 1951), p. 96.

[61]Frank Sorauf, *The Wall of Separation* (Princeton: Princeton University Press, 1976), p. 254.

[62]*Ibid.,* p. 5.

[63]Anthony Tortora, *"Ex Parte* McCardle," *National Review* 32 (19 September 1980):   1140.

[64]403 U.S. 615 (1971).

[65]Wilber Katz, *Religion and American Constitutions* (Evanston, Ill.:   Northwestern University Press, 1963), p. 64.

[66]Sorauf, pp. 320-1 *(supra,* note 61).

[67]Mark Yudof, "Law and Education Research: Past and Future," *New York University Education Quarterly* 11 (Fall 1979), p. 12.

[68]Mark Yudof, "Law and Education Research: Past and Future," *New York University Education Quarterly* 11 (Fall 1979), p. 14.

[69]*Ibid.*, p. 12.

CHAPTER III

THE PUBLIC POLICY QUESTION

Discussions on governmental assistance to nonpublic school parents frequently go nowhere because they begin and end at the same spot: the constitutional issue. This happens for a variety of reasons. First of all, the general population and the legal community alike are divided over the matter. Strong opinions, formed by other considerations, rarely change because of an academic debate. Beginning with the public policy question focuses on whether or not such aid is desirable. If it is desirable, is it legal? If it is desirable but illegal, should the law be changed?

Senator Robert Packwood chided Senator Eagleton for his approach during the tuition tax credit debate of the 95th Congress, because he refused to deal with the public policy issues.[1] Sorauf was concerned with "the community context and group conflict," as well as "the broader policy problems and social attitudes."[2] Abraham also looked at the matter in the same light: "When all is said and done, the issue ultimately falls into the *policy field,* heavily surcharged with considerations of public welfare in a pluralistic society with a democratic base."[3]

That a complex problem requires careful research was stressed by Doyle:

> As the possibility of public support schemes becomes ever more real, it will be necessary to undertake systematic research to begin to assess the probable impact of such funding. Because the debate is passionate, filled with claims and counterclaims about church/state separation, racial and

social class isolation, and academic elitism, a
carefully designed set of research projects could
begin to illuminate some of these questions in a
systematic way. Although research cannot answer
the political question about the appropriateness of
public support, it can help in weighing the impact
of different options.[4]

This chapter was designed to handle some of these questions:

1. Are there precedents for aid?

2. What are the prevalent attitudes toward nonpublic
    schools?

3. How much of the negative attitudes can be accounted
    for by poor information?

4. Is educational competition a benefit for American
    education?

5. Is money a significant issue, or is anti-Catholicism
    a more powerful force in the debate?

6. Would aid contribute to racially segregated
    schools?

7. Has the Supreme Court contravened the wishes of the
    various legislatures?

8. Can one expect significant state control with state
    money?

9. Has the social climate changed on this matter?

10. What is the role of educational pluralism in a
    pluralistic society?

11. Is parental freedom of choice in education a value
    to be pursued and fostered?

Only after these questions have been answered is the constitutional question appropriate to study and discuss.

Precedents for Aid

Opponents of government aid for nonpublic school children sometimes have an inaccurate vision of history. They
assert that no aid has ever been given and, therefore, should
not be given in the future. They fail to realize that "long
after the First Amendment became effective, religion continued to hold a prominent place in public and private education. Public aid to church schools generally increased
until about 1820, and persisted, though on a diminishing
scale, even after the Civil War."[5] Brickman listed specific
examples of state support given directly to the denominational institutions: New York funded charity schools under
religious auspices in 1795; land grants were made to a
Baptist college in 1832 and to a Catholic college in 1833 by
the federal government; the Freedman's Bureau provided
federal funds to Negro schools conducted by religious groups
from 1865 to 1871; the federal government supported Christian
missionary schools in Alaska from 1888 to 1892.[6]

Nor did this assistance cease with the turn of the century, as this list demonstrates: GI Bill of Rights (PL
347); National School Lunch Act of 1946 (PL 396); National
Education Defense Act (PL 85-864); College Aid Act (PL 88-
204); Anti-Poverty Act (PL 88-452); Elementary and Secondary
Education Act (PL 89-10). Packwood saw the first of these
as most significant for the present discussion. He also
called into question the consistency of the federal government and the judicial system.[7]

Blanshard, a long-time opponent of government aid,
defended the GI Bill by saying: "These grants, however,
were made to young people and to veterans not as Catholics
but as needy youths or as veterans of the armed forces."[8]
Ironically enough, long-time supporters of government aid
have used this exact same argument with Blanshard to justify

broader aid programs, namely, that aid is given to a child
in need--without regard to his/her religion or place of
education.

Ample, unbroken precedent does, then, exist.

Public Education v. Private Education

The heading of this section is not accidental; it high-
lights the "us" and "them" attitude that surfaces frequently
in conversations about federal funding for alternatives to
public education. That the public school has achieved a
privileged status can hardly be doubted after reading Justice
William Brennan's concurring opinion in *Lemon v. Kurtzman:*
"This Nation long ago committed itself to primary reliance
upon publicly supported public education to serve its important goals in secular education."[9] Sizer rather sarcasti-
cally referred to the public school as "Mom and apple pie."[10]
Other schools have often been stigmatized as less-than-
desirable and as interlopers. Butts reflected this kind of
thinking.[11] Senator Hodges argued against "creat[ing]
islands,"[12] while Swomley referred to parochial education as
"a rival school system."[13] Senator Chafee reflected a similar insensitivity to children in alternative schools when he
asserted that the Congress has "a particular responsibility
to the youngsters who are attending the public school system
in the United States."[14] This intense protectiveness of the
public schools reached a crescendo when 34 rather disparate
organizations banded together as the National Coalition to
Save Public Education, petitioning Congress to defeat the
tuition tax credit bill.[15]

Parents and teachers in the nonpublic school community
must become aware of this phenomenon and learn how to come
to grips with it. Bishop Spaulding of Peoria in the last
century would seem to have set the pattern well for he

"frequently spoke and wrote on the problems of public education as well, and on their relation to the private religious school, always making clear his strong preference for the latter and yet stating that preference in a manner that avoided alienating fair-minded educators outside his own Church."[16]

Blanshard was concerned that:

> There are a great many communities in which the Catholic schools drain off from the public schools at least one-quarter of the community's children. . . . The separation is particularly harmful when . . . the Catholic group is largely an immigrant group that needs assimilation and Americanization more than any other part of the community.[17]

Blanshard was obviously not the first to come up with this idea for, as the move toward public education education grew, Trinitarian Protestants cooperated in the educational scheme of Massachusetts's Unitarians to use "a centralized public education system as the only means of neutralizing the growing Catholic influx."[18]

Blanshard also warned about possible legislation to assist nonpublic schools parents to exercise freedom of choice:

> If the terms of such an amendment were sufficiently drastic, they might take America back more than a century to the period when our new public schools were fighting for life against sectarian encroachment.[19]

Spaulding's calm rationality would do nothing for such phobia and emotionalism, but it would be reassuring to someone like Berns who expressed a hope that "some scheme might be devised that could provide assistance to church-related schools without injury to the public schools."[20]

Sullivan cautioned that "aid to the nonpublic schools would most likely divert funds from the public schools.

Hence the benefits of any program of aid to the nonpublic schools must be compared with the loss of benefits from the foregone aid to public schools."[21] Senator Anderson of Minnesota offered the experience of his state to those who thought along Sullivan's lines:

> The fact is that during the period of time we had the tuition tax credit in effect, there was *no dramatic* shift out of public education into private education, and in the light of our experience, it appears unlikely that the tuition tax credit would do any damage to public education.[22]

Coons answered objections to parental freedom of choice in this way:

> It [the argument] assumes that, given the chance, anyone with good sense would desert the public schools--that the system survives solely by its capacity for economic incarceration. . . .
> I cannot share this paradoxical view that the brightest hope for the public schools lies in their remaining benign prisons for the lower classes. . . .[23]

Senator Moynihan was alarmed by the fact "that in all the documents and all the statements of the five former commissioners of education considering the future there was no reference of any kind to nonpublic schools."[24] This state of affairs, coupled with the poor statistical data about the private sector held by the National Center for Educational Statistics, led Moynihan to conclude that "the Federal educational establishment does not want to have anything to do with these schools."[25]

Some facts also need more circulation, first in the area of original motivation, and second in the area of current performance. Blumenfeld has argued that the Unitarians opted for publicly controlled schools to create a new climate in America. He went on to suggest that "if Mann was the father of anything, it was of centralized, state-controlled public education, governed by a state bureaucracy, and financed by taxes on property."[26]

As to why teachers favored the public schools movement, the Friedmans have offered some pragmatic reasons:

> They expected to enjoy greater certainty of employment, greater assurance that their salaries would be paid, and a greater degree of control if government rather than parents were the immediate paymaster.[27]

The crisis in confidence in public schools is, according to Glazer, "the product of a failure--the failure to effectively educate the low-income populations of the [public] schools."[28] At the same time, "parochial schools in many cases seem to be doing a better job with less money."[29]

It would not seem rash to suggest that nonpublic school parents will never obtain what they believe to be just until the relationship between the public and private sectors of education improves to the point that a win for one is not automatically perceived as a loss for the other. It is to be hoped that the facts will help the process along and also lead to the removal of "our present monolithic system of education."[30]

Negativity Toward Nonpublic Schools
Due To Misinformation

Much of the negative attitude toward private schools discussed earlier is based on gross misinformation. One of the most basic matters about which people are frequently misinformed involves the origins and practices of church-related schools.

Senator Packwood shared the results of his inquiry into this matter with the Senate:

Last year I wrote to the Library of Congress in my first endeavor to inquire on this subject, and I asked them for a very *brief history of public and church education in this country*, and this is their answer on August 18 last year:

Reference is made to your inquiry of August 10, 1977, requesting information on the above matter, specifically, you ask (1) whether State aid to private church-related schools was a fairly common practice in the United States at least during the first half of the 19th century and (2) whether such aid violated relevant Federal constitutional safeguards.

The answer to these questions is yes and no, respectively.

Yes, to No. 1.   No, to No. 2.

It is a pleasure to get a response to a direct question.[31]

He further inquired about public support for religiously-oriented schools and received the following reply:

In response to your request of January 30, 1978, for a memo regarding the status of schools in America from 1770 to 1820, the following generalization can be made: All, or almost all, the schools during this period were private, were religious, and were publicly supported, that is, denominational schools received public school funds.[32]

Packwood also noted during the course of the tax credit debate one senator who consistently linked the words "public schools and democracy." His observations bear repetition here for the benefit of those who share the impression that democracy can be learned only in public schools:

The two do not necessarily have to be solely intertwined.   There are those people who go to private schools who share some of the beliefs in democracy that those who go to public schools share.

This whole country grew out of private schools. When time and time again we are cited as the founding beacon of democracy in this country it was out of a private school system that it grew, not a public school system.

So, let us not demean those who go to private schools by tying together those words as only those who somehow have their education paid for by public taxes can have the proper view about the way the Government should be run.[33]

Another prevalent image of private schools is that of the elitist academy for the wealthy. This prompted Senator Hollings to refer to them as "those private schools with those endowments."[34] The Senator should be presented with the findings of the study on inner-city private schools conducted by the Catholic League for Religious and Civil Rights. That study put the lie to the impression of non-public schools as havens for white flight or institutions catering to the rich.[35] Walinsky foreshadowed the Catholic League study by declaring that "in the heavily mixed neighborhoods . . . there is more integration within the parochial school than there would be in any school public or private . . ."[36]

Perhaps most incredible of all was Swomley's assertion that "church schools exist only to provide sectarian religious education."[37] Such allegations fly in the face of common knowledge that needs no documentation: that church schools fulfill a dual function of secular and religious education.

If misinformation persists, it is the responsibility of the nonpublic school community to dispel the myths, and for all others to be open to correct information and a corresponding change in attitude and practice. On this score, however, Greeley would not appear too hopeful: "The American educational enterprise does not know much about Catholic schools, but it knows that it is against them."[38]

Decline in Alternate Educational Forms
And the Need for Competition

The decline in nonpublic school enrollment is well known, especially in Catholic schools, and has been documented elsewhere in this study. Senator Packwood reminded his fellow-Senators of the 39% drop in Catholic school enrollment nationwide[39] and urged them to see the tax credit legislation as a means to stave off future declines:

> You will not have any more neighborhood schools that are nonetheless run on alternative bases and provide options to people who have no more than the ordinary opportunities of the ordinary American.
> If you care about those schools, you care about this legislation. If you do not care about those schools, this legislation makes perhaps a marginal claim on your support.[40]

Senator Tower sounded a note of caution about the direction education has taken in recent years in this country:

> We have seen what happens when the State gets a *monopoly on education* in societies and the way things are tending these days. I think that the public schools of the States are coming more and more under the influence of the Central Government. We are going to create the Department of Education. Apparently, I know there are some for it and some against it, and it is an arguable case on both sides. But we could be moving strongly in the direction of centralized, if not controlled, at least very profound influence over public education in this country.
> That makes it, in my view, all the more urgent that we preserve the option for the people in our society in terms of education.[41]

It is not uninteresting to note that Friedman, an economist in the capitalistic tradition who intensely dislikes government doles for any reason, has advocated the voucher system --precisely to break the back of the government monopoly on education.[42] An essay by Friedman spelled out his intent clearly, maintaining that "parents could express their views about schools directly by withdrawing their children from one school and sending them to another, to a much greater extent than is now possible."[43]

An essay by Kenealy strongly stressed the need for "the good old system of American competition between systems having an equal chance to serve the country."[44] Senator Stevens hit upon the element of competition again:

> They are claiming that making private schools more affordable will increase the competition between the two types of institutions by putting them on more equal ground. Mr. President, I support this type of competition and think that it can only serve to better the overall quality of our schools. If the public school administrators truly feel threatened by a $170 credit, then I must assume that their schools are in serious trouble and perhaps parents should disenroll their children.[45]

John Stuart Mill was a most vocal opponent of state-run schools. However, he conceded their necessity on a limited basis for a fascinating reason:

> An education established and controlled by the State should only exist, if it exists at all, as one among many competing experiments, carried on for the purpose of example and stimulus, to keep the others up to a certain standard of excellence.[46]

The day of competition may be on the horizon if Elam's editorial remarks are any indicator of a new mood in the educational establishment:

> Why have elected county superintendents like those in Marin and Contra Costa of California decided to support the Coons plan? Undoubtedly, it is because the public schools in some areas have failed to deliver the services the system promises. The basic questions are: Why have they failed? Would another formula--some version of the voucher plan--more nearly achieve our mutual goals? We will probably never know until and unless the idea is thoroughly tested in practice.[47]

The comments take on deep significance when one realizes
that *Phi Delta Kappan* has not only served as a significant
voice of the educational establishment for years, but has
also been in the forefront of opposition to any form of
governmental assistance to provide alternatives to public
education.   In fact, one could legitimately ask if the
public policy question on the need for genuine competition
in education has already been answered--and in the affirmative, for many believe that "the return of educational
freedom is essential to American freedom in general."[48]

The Budgetary Dimension

The financial question is uppermost in the minds of most
intelligent discussants of the issue of federal aid to nonpublic school parents. Since the specifics of the financial
question are frequently debated in detail elsewhere, and
since the emphasis here is on the philosophical and other
justifications, only a brief treatment has been offered
here.

Proponents of state aid have often been guilty of assuming that the federal well can never run dry because they
have not seen it happen yet. Senator Muskie highlighted the
need for fiscal responsibility in regard to the tax credit
legislation.[49] While one could call him to have a different
set of priorities to avoid deficit spending, and could certainly call him to task for implicitly putting himself in
the position of a middle-income or ghetto parent faced with
tuition, the basic point he made has validity.

The government has its financial problems, but so do the
sponsoring institutions.   In his research on inner-city
Catholic schools, Vitullo-Martin discovered that "a typical
parish spends 70% of its income on its school."[50] Outside
of special fund-raisers, the only other source of income is

tuition and, as the present researcher has noted elsewhere, "we are pricing ourselves out of existence."[51]

Sizer's essay argued that it will be cheaper for the government to aid than to absorb nonpublic school children. He went on to reflect on his guess as to how the problem will be resolved: "The pragmatic American will willy-nilly get over his church-state hang-up. Taxes now seem to be a more telling issue than theology."[52]

A *Newsweek* Poll also discovered that programs like tuition tax credits serve as incentives to public school parents to consider nonpublic schools, thus suggesting a saving of tax dollars rather than a loss.[53]

The Role of Anti-Catholicism in the Debate

Not all who oppose federal aid to nonpublic school parents are anti-Catholic; even some Catholics oppose the notion. However, it is not a misreading of either the past or the present to allege a connection between anti-Catholicism and attitudes opposing parochial school aid. For Higham observed, "The most luxuriant tenacious tradition of paranoic agitation in American history has been anti-Catholicism."[54]

Of the historical link there can be no doubt. Three rather diverse observers can be brought forward in this regard. Katz very bluntly said that the "no aid" position was "associated with successive waves of anti-Catholic feeling."[55] Kraushaar was no less emphatic: "These prohibitions owe their origin to times past when anti-immigrant or anti-Catholic sentiments were rampant."[56] Pfeffer, too, has seen the relationship "because most of these provisions [against state aid to parochial schools] were placed into State constitutions in the 19th Century when anti-Catholic bigotry flourished, and because they were generally applied in the courts against Catholic schools."[57]

The present day is not free from anti-Catholicism, either. Walinsky put it very starkly when he declared that animosity toward parochial school aid plans persists because of "an implicit liberal self-righteousness that treats defeat of Catholic interests as triumphs over the devil."[58] A cursory glance through the list of traditional opponents to federal aid for nonpublic school parents, or through the *Congressional Record* during the tuition tax credit debate, or through many of the opinions of the Supreme Court on this topic will reveal that anti-Catholicism still exists --toned down perhaps, but still not too subtle.

It is somewhat of an anomaly that an organization like the American Civil Liberties Union should always be on the horizon to fight against the civil liberties of Catholic parents. They share this penchant with Americans United for Separation of Church and State (formerly known as "Protestants and Others United . . ."). The behavior of these two powerful groups has led McLaughlin to declare that "these organizations are unflagging in their efforts to prevent public aid of any kind from reaching Catholic schools particularly."[59]

Sorauf's detailed study of Americans United brought many interesting, and usually unnoticed, facts to light:

> To a very surprising degree AU was interested only in those cases in which Roman Catholic interests were involved--cases dealing with bus rides to parochial schools and nuns teaching in public schools, for instance. It is precisely in these figures--AU participated in 72 percent of the cases in which Roman Catholic interests were involved, but in only 7 percent of the other cases--that the suspicions of AU's anti-Catholic animus are most deeply grounded.[60]

Sorauf admitted to some change in AU but went on to maintain that the change is superficial.[61]

The most virulent opponent of the tax credit for elementary and secondary nonpublic school parents was Senator Hollings; it was his amendment that limited the credit to college students in 1978. His anti-Catholicism came out on numerous occasions during the debate and might have left a listener wondering just what was being debated. Let two examples suffice.

His first was an attempt to justify his deletion of elementary and secondary schools from the bill. The remarks were designed to be conciliatory, but devout Catholics or any other people of good will and sensitivity could only have perceived them as inflammatory. The tendency to present Catholic education in a most unfavorable manner was obvious: the education is narrow, dogmatic, hierarchical and racist.[62] If all of this were so, need one doubt that it does not merit consideration, let alone aid?

Similar approaches carried over into the second statement, in which he depicted the constituents of the congressmen as castigating them for supporting the tax credit legislation as originally written:

> 'What in heaven's name happened to you? We sent you to Washington charged with looking out, among other things, for the public's interest and the public's concern. We sure did not tell you to take over the church schools down the street. The priests and the bishop of the parish have control of them. We did not send you down there to take care of private schools. You have gone and doubled the amount of aid--general assistance for the first time and for private schools only--to the private and the parochial schools as compared to what you have given to the poor public school students.'[63]

Once again the technique became one of appealing to latent anti-Catholicism through words like "priests and bishop",

through the implication that only Catholic schools stand to
benefit, through pitting these schools against "the poor
public" schools.

The fact that Hollings's allegations went relatively
unchallenged makes one wonder for how many other Senators he
spoke. Could he have spoken thus of blacks or Jews and gone
unchallenged?

Nor has the Supreme Court itself been innocent of derog-
atory comments about Catholic schools, parents and teachers.
Many of these are analyzed in Chapter VI; however, one
stands out among the rest and requires attention at this
point. In his concurring opinion in the *Lemon* case (403 U.S.
670, 1971), Justice Douglas cited a bitter anti-Catholic
tract as definitive proof for what Catholic education is all
about. Senator Moynihan saw a connection with the whole
debate over tuition tax credits and alleged that the
anti-Catholicism is so ingrained and deep that it goes
unnoticed:

> Madam President, as a member of the community
> of Catholic scholars, I must say that it was most
> extraordinary that this incredible proposition went
> unremarked. Nobody took issue with it. No brother
> judge said 'Surely, Justice Douglas, you did not
> mean to cite that book.'[64]

Senator Ribicoff picked up on a similar angle:

> It seems that the debate is posing a conflict
> between public schools, on one hand, and a mono-
> lithic sectarian system of schools on the other.
> There has been much talk that this bill has been
> designed to take care of Catholic parochial
> schools.[65]

Sorauf's insights were again germane:

> Politically, educationally, and constitution-
> ally, the most important fact about alternatives to
> public education in the United States is that they
> are largely Roman Catholic. . . . It is not much of

an exaggeration to say that the debate over public support for private education in the United States is in fact debate over aid to Catholic Schools.[66]

If Sorauf is correct, the possible options for the future might be three: (1) Anti-Catholicism will be confronted and overcome; (2) Catholic schools will die; (3) Catholic schools will decline while other denominational schools grow, reducing the impact of the Catholic presence in education and simultaneously causing a shift in the discussion to other matters of more substance, scholarship and import, one would hope.

The Racial Issue

Certain opponents of federal assistance to nonpublic school parents have made much of the populations served by public and private schools, respectively. The usual contention is that private schools exclude minorities, cater to the elite, and fail to foster integration. While these accusations are true of the academies operated to avoid desegregation, they are not true of most religiously-oriented schools, and surely not correct in regard to Catholic schools.

The Catholic League study on inner-city private schools, already referred to, clearly demonstrates the Catholic commitment to providing quality education to minorities, even though half of these children in Catholic schools are non-Catholic. This corroborated the findings of Vitullo-Martin on the religious aspect of the question.[67]

Most Catholic schools serve a predominant ethnic group in the cities because they are parochial (that is, parish or neighborhood) schools. Nor do Jewish schools reflect a high degree of racial mix. To blame this situation on the schools themselves is to miss the point that very few minorities would be attracted to a Jewish school because of religious and cultural differences.

Senator Hodges indicated his belief that the tuition tax credit bill would "have strong racial overtones."[68] Senator Stevens explained how the bill excluded segregationist academies and went on to show how it will benefit minorities: "It is clear to me, therefore, that this bill will not foster segregation but will have the opposite effect by increasing the educational opportunities of the less advantaged."[69]

The Friedmans have been strong advocates of a voucher system precisely because "the parents in the suburbs are getting far more value for their tax dollars than the parents in the inner cities."[70] Sowell, the leading black economist and sociologist in America today, has argued along very similar lines.[71]

A Case of Court Over Congress?

In 1957 Corwin charged the Supreme Court with usurping powers and deliberately misreading the original intent of the Constitution it is supposed to interpret.[72] Some observers have regarded the present controversy over state aid not only as an example of Court over Constitution, but also as one of Court over Congress. After listening to dozens of Senators argue that they were powerless to vote counter to the wishes of the Court on this matter, Senator Roth suggested that Congress not take a back seat to the Court, but that both do their respective jobs.[73]

In reality, it is inaccurate to speak of the Court having contravened the wishes of Congress on the aid issue. As a matter of fact, it never has. In the only Supreme Court case concerned with federal legislation to benefit nonpublic school students through Title I, the Court upheld

the legislation in *Wheeler v. Barrera*.[74] The Court has,
however, struck down numerous aid programs which originated
in state legislatures. The Court may have sent up an
unconscious signal as to how proponents of federal aid to
nonpublic school parents should proceed. If the Court is
reluctant to tackle acts of Congress in this area (and this
has not been categorically proven), federal legislative
efforts should take precedence over those at the state
level, whose successes have been marginal at best. Surely
this was behind Valente's thinking in his testimony in
Congressional hearings on the proposed tuition tax credit
legislation in 1978, when he noted that "the Supreme Court
of the United States has always given great deference to
congressional judgments on fiscal policy, and national tax
policy. . . ."[75] It would seem that for such an opinion to
stand up under judicial scrutiny, the Court would have to be
convinced that the challenged legislation was, in fact, a
part of "fiscal policy."

State Control with State Money

An ideological difference divides the nonpublic school
community: the desirability of government monies. Some see
state aid as a panacea; others see it as a curse.

Those who believe private schools deserve public support
do so on the basis that they fulfill a public function.
Parsons saw the issue in very clear-cut terms:

> If they do [serve a public purpose], they are
> worthy of public support in return for the contri-
> bution they make to the state; if they do not per-
> form the same function, then they should immediately
> be deprived of approval under state compulsory-
> education laws.[76]

Swomley cautioned against seeking governmental assistance because "to accept tax funds is to accept some degree

of public control and hence to lose independence."[77]   While
the point is well taken, he does not seem to realize that
private schools already have "some degree of public control"
--and correctly so.   However, this need not cause a school
"to lose independence" or its uniqueness.

Brickman accented the need for consistency here:

> If separation must be full, complete, thorough
> and permanent, then we can seriously call into
> question the practice of state control of secular
> education in parochial schools, which have already
> been adjudged to constitute 'an establishment of
> religion.'[78]

This lack of consistency regarding the identity of
parochial schools approached total absurdity when two governmental agencies reached opposite conclusions, causing a two-
fold harm to the institutions.   The National Labor Relations
Board decided that parochial schools were not sufficiently
religious to be free from their regulations on unionization.
The Supreme Court, on the other hand, has generally regarded
these schools as so tied to ecclesiastical life and authority as to be indistinguishable from the Church itself,
thereby making them ineligible for governmental assistance.
The result was that for liabilities, parochial schools would
be considered "schools"; for assets, they were to be treated
like "churches".   To the Court's credit, it did strike down
the NLRB ruling as beyond the NLRB's jurisdiction.[79]

The issue of state control must be squarely faced, pref-
erably before it is too late to be meaningful.

A Changing Social Consensus

Over 20 years ago, Brickman declared that "any solution
to the church-state problem in education seems to be a function of time and circumstance."[80]   He did not intend this to
sound like a haphazard way of resolving a critical issue; he

was merely reflecting on the socio-political facts of life, namely, that certain issues have their day at certain times. The civil rights movement proves that point.

As has already been mentioned, the mood of the American people has become progressively more favorable to the idea of government aid to nonpublic school parents. Senator Muskie conceded: "I know the polls show Americans favor proposals of this kind. These polls have shown favorable majorities for such bills for all the 20 years the Senate has considered them."[81] Pfeffer made a similar admission: "Orthodox Jewry has completely changed its position and now strongly favors governmental aid."[82] The social scientist will want to know why this is so.

Senator Packwood offered one explanation: "The trend in the last 10 years has been a continuing decline in Catholic enrollment and an increase in the enrollment of Protestant and Jewish primary and secondary schools."[83] In other words, the range of beneficiaries has broadened as other religious groups have established schools.

Secondly, with the growing dissatisfaction with public education, more middle- and lower-income parents have opted for private schools, thus moving the issue higher up "on the nation's education agenda."[84]

Lowell warned that the climate could change for non-public schools, and he brought forward the testimony of history to his fellow-opponents of government aid:

> Had not the separate but equal doctrine stood virtually unquestioned for a century before the Court struck it down in the Brown case in 1954? . . . This was a decision in the light of what the Court took to be a shifting consensus.[85]

If we are indeed in the midst of "a shifting social consensus," Fey's advice would be well to follow: "Each side is organized and should organize. Each has the duty to make

its organizations responsible and to insist that they carry
on the contest within the rules of democratic decision-
making."[86]

Even Madison, called forth as the strongest witness on
behalf of absolute separation of Church and State in his
"Memorial and Remonstrance," would seem to favor this
approach: "A measure of such singular magnitude and deli-
cacy ought not to be imposed without the clearest evidence
that it is called for by the majority of citizens."[87]

The Importance of Pluralism

Pluralism, as applied to American schools, is a new element in educational discussions.   This is so because, for
the first century of the nation's life, pluralism in education was a reality taken for granted.   The second century
saw the rise of the public schools movement, which gradually
became the dominant educational establishment, effectively
keeping other forms to a minimum.   The past twenty years,
and especially the last ten, have witnessed the resurgence
of interest in educational pluralism.

Not every voice has been raised on behalf of giving formal expression to educational pluralism, however.   Conant
spoke out vehemently against alternatives to the public
schools:

> The greater the proportion of our youth who
> fail to attend our public schools and who receive
> their education elsewhere, the greater the threat
> to our democratic unity.   To use taxpayers' money
> to assist private schools is to suggest that
> American society use its own hands to destroy
> itself.[88]

Linking up the previous argument with the Supreme Court's
interpretation of the First Amendment in the *Everson* bus
case, Pfeffer said that it was his "belief that adherence

. . . to the principle of strict separation of church and state best serves the interests of religion, of democratic government and of the people."[89]   However, he never indicated why he thought this was so.

Blanshard argued that "the United States . . . has accepted the thesis that education is the function of the state;"[90]   no logical evidence was offered to support this statement.   It would seem that such proof could come only from a totalitarian state.[91]

Thayer's essay dealt with the question of governmental subsidy to foster educational pluralism. Her conclusion was formed thus:

> To permit the remission of taxes to all who prefer private to public services would commit the state to a principle suicidal in its effects not only upon public education, but upon every service administered by the public at public expense.[92]

Senator Hodges gave contemporary testimony to the survival of the above attitudes. His comments were seasoned with phrases like: "cornerstone of our Republic," "national stability," "melting pot," "strength of America."[93]

The newer (or better, renewed) emphasis on pluralism was reflected in the statements of those who follow, for "pluralism has had a rapid rise in popularity among an increasing number of critics of public education during the past decade or so."[94]   This development should come as no surprise to a social scientist, as Murray suggested 20 years earlier: "One would expect that, as the pattern of society has altered and assumed a new pluralistic structure, so too would the pattern of the school system."[95]   He went on to explain his position more fully:

> We have to do with a segment of our society, fully integrated into its pluralist structure, which has now become so large that its educational

needs and interests have become public needs and
interests, at the same time that they remain special to the particular community. . . . It must be
remembered that the good of a pluralistic society
has to be defined in pluralistic terms.[96]

Australia's recent debates on this topic might well be
"instructive for American public philosophy."[97]

Undoubtedly, Murray would have agreed with Herberg's
suggestion that "the religious school, in our kind of free
society, must be regarded as essentially a public institution, though it is not governmentally sponsored and
operated."[98] Donahue maintained a similar position:

A state school system in intimate contact with
religious schools and exercising partial control
over them would be most realistically in accord
with our pluralistic pattern of handling the
question of religion and state power.[99]

Creegan had an interesting concept of a truly liberal
government: "In practice, true liberalism must subsidize
pluralism and even, in some cases, subsidize a measure of
conflict."[100] Marnell related this notion to American
history and constitutional law:

There was nothing in it [the Constitution] to
define the relations of Church and state, except in
terms of the individual and in terms of its explic-
it prohibition of a congressionally established
church. Eighteenth-century liberals, unlike many
of the twentieth-century, always thought first in
terms of the individual and his rights.[101]

The importance of the individual led Brickman to recall
that:

The state has been making provision for the
education of almost every child--the normal, the
gifted, the mentally retarded, the physically handicapped, and the culturally and linguistically
handicapped, and the culturally and linguistically
disadvantaged. It has not yet undertaken to provide for the education of a child who needs reli-

gious instruction in a religious atmosphere together
with his secular studies. The needs of such a child
are as real to him as other needs are to other
children.[102]

In referring to the famous "Amish exemption", Erickson

pursued Brickman's principles of logic and educational

psychology:

> [T]he approach may be constitutional if viewed, not
> as a set of exceptions for a single sect, but as
> simply one application among many of a universally
> valid principle. To be effective, educational
> programs must be fitted to the cultures of the
> pupils served.[103]

Sullivan showed himself to be in the same school of

thought.[104] Mencken blasted public education's bureaucrats

and accused them of the "degrading standardization which now

afflicts the American people."[105]

Senator after senator rose to argue on behalf of educa-

tional pluralism during the tuition tax credit debate.

Senator De Concini synthesized all the arguments into one:

> Mr. President, I believe that H. R. 12050 is
> consistent with the principles that have guided
> American educational philosophy and policy. In
> my view, pluralism is at the center of all we
> Americans do--it is as central to our educational
> system as it is to our politics and our culture.
> Unlike repressive societies we support and encour-
> age diversity of all sorts. To the extent that
> this legislation will assist an ailing nonpublic
> educational sector, it will also directly contrib-
> ute to a continuation of this vital tradition.
> I personally, would be greatly saddened if the
> ravages of inflation and other economic woes forced
> the closing of private educational institutions.
> Certainly we cannot deny that our public schools
> are among the best in the world, but we are better
> off as a people and a Nation as a result of diver-
> sity in our educational system.[106]

Senator Moynihan zeroed in on the political implications

of a unitary school system, like Blumenfeld, already cited.[107]

The Senate also voted to affix the following Preamble to the tax credit bill as providing the rationale they felt best expressed their attitudes and actions:

> The Congress finds that the existence of diverse public and nonpublic educational institutions of high quality, at the primary, secondary, and postsecondary levels, is important to an educational system suited to the pluralist preferences and aspirations of the American people.[108]

Senator Moynihan summarized eloquently what the whole discussion of educational pluralism is concerned with, and it is nothing less than this fundamental doctrine and mission for America today: "E pluribus unum."[109]

Gordis raised it as *the* question a generation ago: "The real issue that must be met is which interpretation of the classical American doctrine of the separation of church and state is most likely to advance the interests of a free society in the twentieth century?"[110] Moynihan, De Concini, and others like them believe they have found the answer.

Parental Freedom of Choice

Perhaps the most important aspect of the question of parental freedom of choice in education is that the focus has been shifted from a discussion of giving government money to men in miters[111] to an analysis of whether or not parental choice is a value to be pursued and, if so, how that value can then be maximized. A special area of concern is how to heighten parental choice for the poor, particularly in this age of sensitivity toward minorities for, as Blum has observed, "the greatest degradation of poverty is the unavailability of choice."[112]

Article 26 of the Universal Declaration of Human Rights of the United National Charter deals with the matter of education, indicating that it is a basic right of every person and is to be free and compulsory, at least at the elementary level. Article 26 goes on to assert that: "Parents have a prior right to choose the kind of education that shall be given to their children."[113] Putting the two statements together, one could justifiably raise the question as to whether the present practice of the United States is in violation of the United Nations Charter.

The Fathers of the Second Vatican Council, in their Declaration on Religious Freedom, addressed the same issue when they said:

> Government, in consequence, must acknowledge the right of parents to make a genuinely free choice of schools and of other means of education. The use of this freedom of choice is not to be made a reason for imposing unjust burdens on parents, whether directly or indirectly.[114]

A similar treatment of the matter was presented in their Declaration on Christian Education, already alluded to in this study.

Pope John Paul II, in speaking to UNESCO officials in Paris, combined the rationale of both the U.N. and Vatican II statements to renew his, and the Church's, defense of the primacy of parental and familial rights:

> Allow me to claim in this place for Catholic families the right which belongs to all families to educate their children in schools which correspond to their view of the world, and in particular the strict right of Christian parents not to see their children subjected, in schools, to programs inspired by atheism. That is, indeed, one of the fundamental rights of man and of the family.[115]

In his letter to the signatory countries of the Helsinki Accords, John Paul again presented parental freedom of choice in education as a fundamental freedom, which could not have a price tag attached to it.[116]

These arguments are not novel; the philosophers have repeated them many times over. Mill, greatly opposed to governmental intervention in education, conceded only this role to government: "It might leave to parents to obtain the education where and how they pleased, and content itself with helping to pay the school fees of the poorer classes of children."[117]

Maritain was no less forceful in his denunciation of a government that interposed itself between parent and child:

> But the State becomes iniquitous and tyrannical if it claims to base the functioning of civil life on forced labor, or if it tries to violate the rights of the family in order to become master of men's souls . . . man is constituted a part of family society before being constituted a part of political society.[118]

If it is true that religious leaders and philosophers have been saying these things for generations and even centuries, how could parental freedom of choice be considered a new element in the context of this study? Only because the arguments on behalf of this are now being heard and accepted in the public forum and in the political arena. Let the testimony of several senators who participated in the tax credit debate of 1978 serve as witness to this new attitude of acceptance. Honesty would require admission that this position did not have universal acceptance, as Senator Bentsen's remarks illustrated.[119] While the Senator admitted the right to choose, he did not see how it is contingent on the ability to pay. His example of swimming pools was a further indication of a lack of philosophical and practical knowledge, namely, that swimming is not required by law while attendance at school is. However, it is important to note that his was one of the few voices raised against this aspect of the public policy question.

Senator Roth saw clearly what Senator Bentsen could not see and had this to say:

> But as the sharp drop in nonpublic school enrollment shows, too many parents no longer have a freedom of choice. In fact, more and more parents are being deprived of the freedom of choice to send their children to nonpublic schools by a government which takes more of their earnings through higher taxes and inflation.
> I believe a tuition tax credit will restore freedom of choice to the millions of American families who are struggling to pay both school tuition and higher taxes for public schools.[120]

However, a recurring criticism of the tax credit legislation was that only the wealthy would benefit. Senator De Concini responded by documenting the fact that the prime beneficiaries would be middle-income parents.[121]

Senator Stevens identified the constituency of private schools and concluded that:

> [W]ith a 13-percent drop in nonpublic school enrollment, the middle-income student is again the one most affected. Private schools primarily educate the lower and middle income groups with 71 percent of private school students coming from families with incomes below $25,000. Fewer than 4 percent of those attending private schools have incomes greater than $50,000.[122]

Stevens's statistics squared off with Vitullo-Martin's information on this score.

Vitullo-Martin discovered that 57% of all private school students in New Mexico are from minority groups.[123] Schmitt's statement took on new meaning in the light of the statistic just cited. He disclosed:

> When I contacted Hispanic groups in New Mexico to inquire as to their feelings about tuition tax credit, the response was enthusiastically in support of this proposal. I was told that any proposal which aided education, which gave parents more control over the education of their children,

and which prompted competition and choice in education was welcome. These groups, some of which are
involved in education, understand that minorities
stand to benefit the most under this bill and not
at the cost of some other groups.[124]

He then went on to analyze the entire question, effectively
touching on the key elements of the issue: parental choice,
educational competition, and the constitutional question.[125]
His reference to family choice found echoes in English's comment that he happens "to respect the integrity and freedom of
the family."[126] Schmitt's last point received an in-depth
treatment in the chapter of this work devoted to the constitutional dimension of the matter.

One of the most eloquent speeches on the critical importance of parental freedom of choice in education was delivered by Senator Hayakawa. No stranger to the educational
community, he has served at the University of Chicago and
San Francisco State University. His testimony thus had a
two-fold impact coming as it did from an educator and a
legislator. His remarks have been quoted below *in toto* because of their comprehensive nature and because the speech
is quite brief--as senatorial colloquies go.[127] The conclusion of Hayakawa's impassioned plea was that the senators
take their "stand in defense of parental rights and educational freedom."

A Summary of the Public Policy Question

While this chapter has considered over a dozen sides of
the public policy question whether nonpublic school parents
merit federal financial assistance, the last two sections
(on the importance of pluralism and parental freedom of
choice) contain the truly critical issues to be resolved for
any democratic nation. All the others are simply parts of
these two broader matters.

The importance of pluralism in education cannot be overstated if a nation is to prosper and grow in the ways of freedom. A mere external conformity does not ensure unity of spirit. Poland stands out as a powerful and no longer silent reminder of this fact.

Parental freedom of choice is a sacred right, upheld in philosophy, theology and law--yet a meaningless commodity to millions of Americans because they lack the financial wherewithal to exercise it for themselves and their children. Parental rights are basic human rights and one thread that is, in many ways, responsible for keeping the whole fabric of liberty in one piece.

The public policy question, then, revolves around the desire of this nation to foster a genuine pluralism in education and genuine freedom for parents to select that educational form that best reflects their values and the values they want transmitted to their children. The question to be answered is: Can federal financial assistance to nonpublic school parents accomplish this?

NOTES

CHAPTER III

[1]"It is those policy reasons we have tried to argue, and argued in vain, because we kept getting back to the *constitutional argument*.
"If the Senator is, indeed, opposed on policy positions, I would love to argue that topic because I found time and again people hiding behind the constitutional argument because they did not want to talk about the *policy issues* implicit in this legislation."
[95th Congress, p. 13319.]

[2]Frank Sorauf, *The Wall of Separation* (Princeton: Princeton University Press, 1976), p. 5.

[3]Henry Abraham, *Freedom and the Court* (New York: Oxford University Press, 1976), p. 271.

[4]Denis Doyle, "Public Policy and Private Education," *Phi Delta Kappan* 62 (September 1980): 17.

[5]Otto Krauschaar, *American Nonpublic Schools* (Baltimore: Johns Hopkins University Press, 1972), p. 20.

[6]William Brickman, *Subsidized Pluralism in American Education* (New York: Society for the Advancement of Education, 1959), p. 113.

[7]"It is interesting that in the GI bill, the Veterans' educational benefits bill, payments will be made to the following educational institutions: Any public or private elementary school, secondary school, vocational school, correspondence school, business school, junior college, teachers college, normal school, professional school, university, scientific or technical institution, and this is constitutional.
"We have checked with the VA. They have made payments to primary and secondary sectarian schools under the GI bill of rights, along with public schools, primary and secondary, under the GI bill.
"There must be an assumption that the ones who have gone through the military service have been indoctrinated that any kind of religious school payments are safe. In this case they are payments to the institution, not payments to the individual on behalf of the institution but to the institution. So by the time, as we have said earlier, you are allowed to make payments to the church to take care of your preschool children until they are 6, you are entitled to make payments to colleges, public and private, if you are a veteran you are entitled to have payments made to primary and secondary schools, it is a very

narrow group that seems susceptible to being unduly influenced by religion."
[95th Congress, p. 13238.]

[8]Paul Blanshard, *American Freedom and Catholic Power* (Boston: Beacon Press, 1960), p. 113.

[9]403 U.S. 658 (1971).

[10]Theodore Sizer, "Education and Assimilation," *Phi Delta Kappan* 58 (September 1976): 30.

[11]R. Freeman Butts, "Education Vouchers, *Phi Delta Kappan* 61 (September 1979): 7.

[12]95th Congress, p. 13329.

[13]John Swomley, *Religion, the State and the Schools* (New York: Pegasus Books, 1968), p. 92.

[14]95th Congress, p. 13240.

[15]*Ibid.*, p. 13209.

[16]David Sweeney, *The Life of John Lancaster Spaulding* (New York: Herder and Herder, 1966), p. 16.

[17]Paul Blanshard, *American Freedom and Catholic Power* (Boston: Beacon Press, 1960), p. 80.

[18]Samuel Blumenfeld, *Is Public Education Necessary?* (Old Greenwich, Ct.: Devin-Adair Co., 1981), p. 241.

[19]Paul Blanshard, *Religion and the Schools* (Boston: Beacon Press, 1963), p. 169.

[20]Walter Berns, *The First Amendment and the Future of American Democracy* (New York: Basic Books, 1976), p. 74.

[21]Daniel Sullivan, *Public Aid to Nonpublic Schools* (Lexington, Mass.: Heath and Co., 1974), p. 102.

[22]95th Congress, p. 13348.

[23]John Coons, "Of Family Choice and 'Public' Education," *Phi Delta Kappan* 61 (September 1979): 13.

[24]95th Congress, p. 13195.

[25]95th Congress, p. 13241.

[26]Blumenfeld, p. 184 *(supra,* note 18).

[27]Milton & Rose Friedman, *Free to Choose* (New York: Avon Books, 1981), p. 143.

[28]Nathan Glazer, "Ethnicity and Education: Some Hard Questions," *Phi Delta Kappan* 63 (January 1981):   388.

[29]David Savage, "Expect a Battle over Tuition Tax Credits," *Phi Delta Kappan* 63 (February 1981):   411.

[30]Elmer Thiessen and Ray Wilson, "Curriculum in the Church-State Controversy," *Inform* 3 (January 1981):   7.

[31]95th Congress, p. 13202.

[32]*Ibid.*

[33]*Ibid.,* p. 13329.

[34]*Ibid.,* p. 13213.

[35]See: Timothy O'Brien and Donald Zewe, "Hope in the Inner City," *Momentum* 12 (February 1981):   11-13.

[36]Adam Walinsky, "Aid to Parochial Schools," *New Republic* 166 (7 October 1972):   19.

[37]Swomley, p. 109 *(supra,* note 13).

[38]Andrew M. Greeley, *An Ugly Little Secret* (Kansas City: Sheed, Andrews & McMeel, 1977), p. 79.

[39]95th Congress, p. 13242.

[40]*Ibid.*

[41]*Ibid.,* p. 13201.

[42]Milton Friedman, *Capitalism and Freedom* (Chicago: University of Chicago Press, 1972), p. 85.

[43]George LaNoue, ed., *Education Vouchers: Concepts and Controversies* (New York: Teachers College Press, 1972), p. 13.

[44]Thomas O'Toole, ed., *Institute of Church and State* 2 (Villanova, Pa.: Villanova University School of Law, 1959), p. 109.

[45]95th Congress, p. 13256.

[46]John Stuart Mill, *On Liberty* (New York: Henry Holt & Company Publishers, 1898), p. 184.

[47]Stanley Elam, "The Passing Parade," *Phi Delta Kappan* 62 (November 1980): 163.

[48]Blumenfeld, p. 249 *(supra,* note 18).

[49]"I have 5 children of my own. I have paid my share of tuition bills. But our responsibility, Mr. President, goes beyond responding to the popular causes of the moment. We are talking here about enacting a tax credit bill which would add more than $5 billion a year to the deficit within 5 years. Even little junior would cost nearly $3 billion every year within 5 years, and that assumes we can stunt his growth." [95th Congress, p. 13244.]

[50]Thomas Vitullo-Martin, *Catholic Inner-City Schools* (Washington: United States Catholic Conference, 1979), p. 180.

[51]Peter M. J. Stravinskas, "Parents and Schools: The Right to Choose," an address to the Paterson Diocesan Home-School Federation, 5 October 1980, p. 4

[52]Sizer, p. 27 *(supra,* note 10).

[53]See: Denis A. Williams, "The Bright Flight," *Newsweek* 97 (20 April 1981): 66-73.

[54]John Higham, *Send These To Me* (New York: Atheneum Press), 1975, p. 68.

[55]Wilber Katz, *Religion and American Constitutions* (Evanston, Ill.: Northwestern University Press, 1963), p. 64.

[56]Krauschaar, p. 290 *(supra,* note 5).

[57]Leo Pfeffer, *God, Caesar and the Constitution* (Boston: Beacon Press, 1975), p. 257.

[58]Walinsky, p. 19 *(supra,* note 36).

[59]Sr. M. Raymond McLaughlin, *The Liberty of Choice* (Collegeville, Minn.: Liturgical Press, 1979), p. 151.

[60]Sorauf, p. 60 *(supra,* note 2).

[61]"And yet AU does retain some of the old shrill anti-Catholic tone; it still appeals (however covertly and through 'code' phrases such as 'Spain') to fears of Catholicism rather than to a separationist commitment. And even into the 1970's the editorials of *Church and State,* the AU Magazine, retain a fondness for pictures of public officials kissing episcopal rings."
[*Ibid.,* p. 34.]

[62]"If you look at the makeup of the student body in these schools of higher learning there is a tremendous diversity coming from all walks of life. You will not find that in the little parochial school of the Catholic Church.

"This is not *anti-Catholicism,* but these are facts. Some church leaders speak of it as a mortal sin, in some parishes still today, if you do not send your child to a Catholic school in order to be taught and inculcated with the principles and faith of the Catholic dogma.

"There we are. It is a religious belief. The overwhelming percentage of students attending the Catholic schools are made up of Catholics, at the elementary and secondary level, and this vast majority of little Catholic children are responding to the teaching of the Church. Whom are they taught by? The Senator cannot see the difference with a Lutheran college? In the Catholic school level, they are taught by the various *priests* and *nuns.* Over the years that is the way they have taught their school.

"I have a diversity of employees in my own Senate office. One young lady as we were talking about this last week said, 'Well, I attended Catholic schools both at the elementary and secondary level. It was supposed to be integrated. But not one black child attended that school while I was in the Catholic schools.'" (Emphasis added)
[95th Congress, p. 13210.]

[63]*Ibid.,* p. 13347.

[64]*Ibid.,* p. 13323.

[65]*Ibid.,* p. 13249.

[66]Sorauf, pp. 320-321 *(supra,* note 2).

[67]Vitullo-Martin, p. 93 *(supra,* note 50).

[68]95th Congress, p. 13356.

[69]*Ibid.,* p. 13256.

[70]Friedman & Friedman, p. 148 *(supra,* note 27).

[71]See: Thomas Sowell, "Patterns of Black Excellence," Supplement to
the *Catholic League Newsletter,* August 1976.

[72]See: Edward Corwin, *Court over Constitution* (Gloucester, Mass.:
Peter Smith Publishers, 1957).

[73]"I do not believe Congress should not act on an issue merely
because some scholars believe the Supreme Court may rule it unconstitutional. It is about time that Congress recognize it is a coequal branch
of government, and I believe we should act and allow the Court to rule
on the issue."
[95th Congress, p. 13341.]

[74]417 U.S. 402 (1974).

[75]William Valente before the Committee on Ways and Means, *Tax Treatment of Tuition Expenses* (Washington: U.S. Government Printing Office,
1978), p. 231.

[76]Wilfrid Parsons, *The First Freedom* (New York: Declan McMullen
Co., 1948), p. 125.

[77]Swomley, p. 111 *(supra,* note 13).

[78]Brickman, p. 117 *(supra,* note 6).

[79]77 U.S. 752 (1979).

[80]Brickman, p. 245 *(supra,* note 6).

[81]95th Congress, p. 13244.

[82]Pfeffer, *God, Caesar and the Constitution,* p. 10.

[83]95th Congress, p. 13310.

[84]Doyle, p. 17 *(supra,* note 4).

[85]C. Stanley Lowell, *The Church-State Fraud* (New York: Robert Luce,
Inc., 1973), p. 112.

[86]Dallin Oaks, ed., *The Wall between Church and State* (Chicago:
University of Chicago Press, 1963), p. 34.

[87]John Wilson, *Church and State in American History* (Englewood,
N.J.: Heath & Co., 1965), p. 72.

[88]James Conant, *Education and Liberty* (Cambridge, Mass.: Harvard University Press, 1953), p. 81.

[89]John Cogley, ed., *Religion in America* (New York: Meridian Books, 1958), p. 57.

[90]Blanshard, 1963, p. 193 *(supra,* note 8).

[91]"The simple truth that experience has taught us is that the most potent and significant expression of statism is a State educational system. Without it, statism is impossible. With it, the State can, and has, become everything."
[Samuel Blumenfeld, "Why the Schools Went Public," *Reason* 10 (March 1979): 23.]

[92]William Brickman and Stanley Lehrer, eds., *Religion, Government and Education* (New York: Society for the Advancement of Education, 1961), p. 37.

[93]"Yet the American public school system is a cornerstone of our Republic. It has contributed mightly [sic] to national stability, to equality, to greatness. For roughly 150 years our public schools have demonstrated a method of achieving an enlightened and unified citizenry, in assisting the children of those coming to our shores from different lands, from various cultures and religious backgrounds, speaking different languages, and of different intellectual qualities, to become united into one nation. This is part of the traditional melting pot.
"Therefore, it would seem reasonable to me that its preservation should be of vital concern to all Americans.
"The sense of community closeness, or equality, is bound to be developed when children attend school together for a period of 12 years, beginning in early childhood. To me this is part of the strength of America; and providing subsidies to encourage parents to remove their children from the public schools will tend to diminish this unity and this strength."
[95th Congress, p. 13337.]

[94]Butts, p. 10 *(supra,* note 11).

[95]J. C. Murray, *We Hold These Truths* (New York: Sheed & Ward, 1960), p. 147.

[96]*Ibid.,* pp. 147-8.

[97]"A Lesson from Australia," *America* 144 (18 April 1981): 310.

[98]Cogley, p. 125 *(supra,* note 88).

[99]Brickman, p. 256 *(supra,* note 6).

[100]Robert Creegan, "Subsidized Pluralism," *Schools and Society* 86 (January 1958): 34.

[101]William Marnell, *The First Amendment* (Garden City, N.Y.: Doubleday, 1966), p. 103.

[102]Virgil Blum, *Freedom in Education* (Garden City, N.Y.: Doubleday, 1965), p. 10.

[103]Donald Erickson, *Public Controls for Nonpublic Schools* (Chicago: University of Chicago Press, 1969), p. 52.

[104]See: Sullivan, p. 12 *(supra,* note 21).

[105]"H. L. Mencken Looks at Public Education," *Inform* 3 (March 1981): 1-4.

[106]95th Congress, p. 13243.

[107]"You will find a single educational system in any country where you will find a single political party, and the reverse is equally applicable: Any country that has more than one party has more than one system of education. It is an aspect of the liberty of this society. It is something of value that ought to be preserved."
[95th Congress, p. 13251.]

[108]*Ibid.,* p. 13249.

[109]*Ibid.,* p. 13251.

[110]Robert Gordis, et al., *Religion and the Schools* (New York: Fund for the Republic, 1959), p. 9.

[111]See: Edd Doerr, *Parochiaid and the Law* (Silver Spring, Md.: Americans United for Separation of Church and State, 1970).

[112]Virgil Blum, "Tax Refunds for Tuition," *America* 144 (11 April 1981): 297.

[113]Committee on Human Rights, *For All Humanity* (New York: American Jewish Committee and United Nations Association, 1966), pp. 41-2.

[114]Abbott and Gallagher, eds., *The Documents of Vatican II* (New York: Guild Press, 1966), p. 683.

[115]Pope John Paul II, "Man's Entire Humanity Is Expressed in Culture," *France: Message of Peace, Trust, Love and Faith* (Boston: St. Paul Editions, 1980), p. 202.

[116]". . . freedom for families to choose the schools or other means which provide this sort of education for their children, without having to sustain directly or indirectly extra charges which would in fact deny them this freedom. . . ."
[John Paul II, "Freedom of Conscience and of Religion," *l'Osservatore Romano*, 19 January 1981, p. 13.]

[117]Mill, p. 187 *(supra,* note 46).

[118]Jacques Maritain, *The Rights of Man and Natural Law* (New York: Scribner's 1947), pp. 78-9.

[119]"Mr. President, no one is going to quarrel with the right of a parent to be able to send his child to a private school, just as no one is going to quarrel with the right of a private citizen if he does not want to attend the public pools. While no one is required to swim in the public swimming pools, taxpayers should not have to finance a person's private pool. The right of choice is inherent in everything we stand for in this nation."
[95th Congress, p. 13340.]

[120]*Ibid.,* p. 13341.

[121]"Mr. President, one of the criticisms being levied against this proposed legislation is that the benefits will go primarily to the well-to-do. I respectfully disagree with those who make this charge. According to the Joint Committee on Taxation, 78 percent of the benefits of tuition tax credits would go to families earning less than $30,000 a year. The bulk of the benefits (55 percent) would go to middle-income families earning between $10,000 and $30,000 a year."
[95th Congress, p. 13243.]

[122]*Ibid.,* p. 13255.

[123]Vitullo-Martin, p. 3 *(supra,* note 50).

[124]95th Congress, p. 13352.

[125]"The typical American answer is to increase the incentives for providing a good education. Many of us believe this can be done by the tuition tax credit, a simple way of increasing the range of choice available to parents for the education of their children. With increased freedom of choice comes increased competition among schools to become the beneficiaries of that choice. With competition comes

improvement of the education service being offered whether it be public or private.

"The argument is raised that providing a tax credit for private education, some of which is church affiliated, is unconstitutional. This question must be answered by the courts; but I ask you, how can an increase in the freedom of choice be unconstitutional in a Nation created to preserve freedom of choice?"
[95th Congress, p. 13352.]

[126]Raymond English, "For Tuition Tax Credits and Vouchers," *New York Times* 19 April 1981, p. E15.

[127]"Mr. President, the last time I spoke on the floor about tuition tax credits, my remarks concerned the rights of minority students and their parents to utilize education as a means of personal liberation from poverty and racism. I want to express my appreciation to our colleagues, Senator Packwood and Senator Moynihan, for their kind appraisal of my speech that day and for their distribution of it to other congressional offices. It is a pleasant surprise to find one's intellectual currency in circulation.

"As an advocate of tuition tax credit, especially at the elementary and secondary level, I realize that my remarks will draw criticism as well as approval. We have heard dire warnings that, if we give parents control of their children's education, the public schools of America will close their doors and, one presumes, be turned into warehouses. This is nonsense! I, for one, have more faith in public education than to presume that a little bit of competition would finish it off.

"This has been a rough issue. The lobbyists have come out of the woodwork. The heavy hand of the National Education Associaton—what a name; you would think it were something more than a self-interested union—has attempted to stifle the facts with smokescreens about the Constitution, about segregation, and about costs. And one by one, the winds of change have blown away their obfuscations.

"But that does not make it easier to take a stand on principle and support tuition tax credit in the face of rigorous political opposition.

"Let us make no mistake about it: There will be a price to pay if we stand up for the parents and children of America. Some interest groups will never forgive us for doing that. Their political action committees will target us, and their membership will be instructed to knock us off at the polls. But so what? What, after all, are we here for?

"I will not rehearse again today all the arguments in favor of tuition tax credits. We all know them by heart. Are they constitutional? Ask Billy Graham or Antonin Scalia, our former Assistant Attorney General. Would they help minorities and the poor? Ask Prof. James Coleman and the Harlem Parents Union.

"Let us look beyond the pressure groups. Let us look toward an America which trusts its citizens enough to permit them their own

choices.   Let us look toward the day when poor kids have the same
latitude in education as the children of the Members of Congress.   Let
us   take   our   stand   in   defense   of   parental   rights   and   educational
freedom."
     [95th Congress, p. 13347.]

CHAPTER IV

THE CONSTITUTIONAL QUESTION

Supporters and opponents of state aid to parochial schools seem to have at least one area of agreement, and that is that both sides believe that the Supreme Court of the United States has done violence to the First Amendment either by denying some types of benefits to parochial school children or by permitting other types. The general tenor of contributors to this area of concern has been well summarized by this editorial comment in *America*:

> Two thousand years from now a team of archaeologists from an outer-space colony may excavate a kitchen midden on the site of the United States Supreme Court building amid the ruins of what had once been the city of Washington, D.C. If they come upon a collection of opinions in cases decided under the first section of the First Amendment, will these diggers be able to reconstruct that clause if its text is nowhere given in the bale of documents? Not in a millenium. From details of litigation dealing, for instance, with bus rides for children in nonpublic schools or with the refusal of Jehovah's Witnesses to salute a classroom flag, those busy scholars of the future are not likely to distill these sixteen words: Congress shall make no law respecting an establishment of religion, or prohibiting the free exercise thereof. . . .[1]

This is not an easy topic to study because it is a subject which is highly charged in the emotional domain. It is difficult to find dispassionate discussions, even among scholars, because even they have intense feelings and strong opinions on this matter. The methodology of this chapter has been to examine the issue and provide background from

four vantage points by referring to the relevant literature.
The first consideration was an attempt to exegete the First
Amendment in terms of its language and intent. The second
phase of the analysis centered on the derivative doctrine of
separation of Church and State. A third matter of interest
was to determine the range of opinion on how the Court
should handle conflicts between the "free exercise" and
"establishment" clauses of the First Amendment. A final
line of investigation was concerned with how this nation has
lived with the First Amendment for the nearly two centuries
of its life, especially as it relates to the way opinions of
the Supreme Court have affected educational freedom of
choice for nonpublic school parents.

The Religion Clauses of the First Amendment

     The very essence of the debate over governmental assist-
ance to nonpublic school parents revolves around the meaning
assigned to the expression "establishment of religion". In
many of the Supreme Court decisions, "establishment of
religion" has been equated with "religious establishment".
If the Court has been correct in asserting that the two
terms are synonymous, then the discussion would, of necessity, die. However, many legal scholars have taken serious
exception to this interpretation.

     Kenealy declared that "an establishment of religion
means the official erection of one religion into a preferred
position by law."[2] In a similar vein, Coleman in the same
work maintained that the establishment clause of the First
Amendment "reflects the feeling formed in this country that
one of the important things to avoid was a situation in
which one religion became a government-sponsored religion."[3]
In the *McCollum* case,[4] which dealt with religious instruc-

tion in public schools, the justices rejected these explanations of establishment. O'Neill, however, observed:

> They based their case on the claim that their
> new doctrine is what the First Amendment means and
> was designed to mean by Jefferson, Madison and the
> other Founding Fathers. The validity of the Supreme
> Court position in the McCollum case rests *in toto* on
> the validity of this claim. My position is that
> this claim is given all the respect to which it is
> entitled when it is labeled semantic and historical
> nonsense.[5]

An examination of the *Congressional Record* tended to give
credibility to the position taken by O'Neill. The various
versions proposed and debated gave an inkling of the rationale behind the amendment:

Committee:	No religion shall be established by law. . . .
House:	Congress shall make no law establishing religion.
Senate:	Congress shall make no law establishing articles of faith or a mode of worship.
Madison:	. . . nor shall any national religion be established.

The same document also revealed Madison's personal understanding of the First Amendment's meaning: "That Congress
should not establish a religion, and enforce the legal
observation of it by law, or compel men to worship God in
any manner contrary to their conscience."[6]

Basing his opinion on these proposals and commentaries
on the First Amendment and the method of ascertaining intent
prescribed by the justices in the *McCollum* case, Emerson
remarked that "the meaning and significance of the First
Amendment to the people of the new nation is to be found in
the existing law of England and the colonies."[7] That situa-

tion, of course, was one of having a national church. Howe
has suggested that "among the sacred traditions of American
constitutional law is one which tells us that the principal
responsibility of judges is to carry out the 'intention' of
those who framed the constitution."[8] According to Sobran,
the "Framers were opening the way to multiple religious
influences on the state, rather than prohibiting them all.
The point was to prevent one church from having an automatic
advantage over the others. This should increase, not diminish the influence of faith on our public life."[9]

No discussion of the history of the First Amendment
would be complete without reference to Thomas Jefferson,
usually offered as the strongest opponent to government aid.
For this reason Senator Packwood, during the tax credit
debate of the 95th Congress, presented what he considered to
be evidence of Jefferson's support of his proposed legislation. He said:

> Let the record show that when Thomas Jefferson
> was president, he submitted to the senate in 1803 a
> treaty concluded with the Kaskaskia Indians, and a
> part of that treaty reads as follows:
> And whereas the greater part of said tribe have
> been baptized and received into the Catholic Church
> to which they are attached, the United States will
> give annually, for seven years one hundred dollars
> toward the support of a priest of that religion,
> who will engage to perform for said tribe the
> duties of his office, and also to instruct as many
> of their children as possible, in the rudiments of
> literature, and the United States will further give
> the sum of three hundred dollars, to assist the
> said tribe in the erection of a church.
> Mr. President, those are not the writings and
> that is not the treaty of a man who says that you
> cannot use public funds for private sectarian
> education.[10]

These facts become all the more interesting when one
realizes that Jefferson has been described by his authorita-

tive biographer as "anticlerical and antidoctrinal,"[11] to the point of being "obsessive"[12] in this regard.

However, not everyone agrees that attempting to determine the original intent of the framers is a valid procedure. Black noted that "the textual method, in some cases, forces us to blur the focus and talk evasively."[13] Kauper has argued that there are "difficulties in using Madison and Jefferson as authoritative interpreters of the . . . First Amendment."[14] Pfeffer has added his belief that "this sanctification for all ages of a specific desire of the original framers smacks of ancestor worship."

Nor has the Supreme Court itself been helpful on this score in its vacillation from case to case between these two methodologies of interpretation. In *Quick Bear v. Leupp,* which dealt with the use of Indian funds for parochial schools, the justices ruled that the First Amendment of itself was insufficient to outlaw continuance of the practice:

> Some reference is made to the Constitution, in
> respect to this contract with the Board of Catholic
> Indian missions. It is not contended that it is
> unconstitutional, and it could not be. But it is
> contended that the spirit of the Constitution
> requires that the declaration of policy that the
> government 'shall make no appropriation whatever
> for education in any sectarian schools' should be
> treated as applicable.[16]

Similarly, Smith observed that in the *Everson* case, the Court "found it impossible to answer the specific question put to it on the basis of the First Amendment alone, but made its judgment with the aid of the concept of separation of Church and State."[17] Furthermore, Freund observed that "the accuracy and sufficiency of Mr. Justice Rutledge's examination of history which produced the First Amendment have ,been questioned by scholars, theologians, polemicists

and judges."[18]   In seconding that charge, Corwin noted that
"the question arises, how far a court is entitled to indulge
in bad history and bad logic without having its good faith
challenged."[19]

Still another question to ask is whether the First
Amendment is applicable to the states at all. This question
may surprise some readers, but a close and careful reading of the Amendment, along with a knowledge of colonial
history, reveal a great deal. First, it is Congress that is
to make no law respecting an establishment of religion, thus
leaving the matter open at the state level. Therefore, many
states continued their established churches long after ratification of the First Amendment. Thus Katz remarked that
"this considerably reduces the force of the textual argument
for the broad 'no aid' interpretation."[20]

Constitutional experts are in general agreement that the
First Amendment has been made applicable to the several
states by judicial incorporation.[21]   However, some legal
scholars have suggested that this process was not a wholesale incorporation for the states. Katz has asserted that
"the prevailing view is that the Bill of Rights is imposed
on the states only to the extent of the essentials of a
system of ordered liberty."[22]   Corwin highlighted the same
point: "It is only *liberty* that the Fourteenth Amendment
protects."[23]   If Katz and Corwin are correct, the individual states could legitimately establish churches but could
not infringe a citizen's right to free exercise of religion.
Thus the several states would, in that view, not be bound by
the restrictive "no establishment" clause but are bound by
the "free exercise" clause since it is related to freedom.

A final consideration is whether or not the establishment clause categorically rules out governmental assistance
to parochial schools. Katz has cautiously observed that

"it is by no means clear that the 'no establishment' clause forbids inclusion of religious schools in general aid programs."[24]   Drinan made a far more forceful statement: "The state . . . can comply with the First Amendment if it makes available funds for strictly secular purposes in *all* schools."[25]   Blum would certainly concur in Drinan's opinion:

> The decisive question is not *who* is entrusted with the expenditure of public funds, but for *what* purpose public funds are expended.   If the purpose is a *public* purpose, it matters not that the agency which spends the money is private or church-related.[26]

Kauper, in commenting on the *Zorach* case, interpreted the situation in this manner:

> The Court says that the legislature may take account of the religious interests of its people in its legislative program so long as it does not act with coercive effect upon dissenters and non-believers and no preference is given to any one religious group.[27]

The Court has appeared to accept the line of reasoning suggested above, as indicated by its opinion in *Abington v. Schempp:* "To withstand the strictures of the Establishment Clause there must be a secular legislative purpose and a primary effect that neither advances nor inhibits religion."[28]   However, in *Committee for Public Education and Religious Liberty v. Nyquist,* the Court took a more restrictive stance and so Justice Byron White, in a dissenting opinion, felt compelled to remind his brother justices that "the test is one of 'primary' effect, not *any* effect."[29] Pfeffer attacked any such attempt at a carefully nuanced interpretation of the First Amendment: "I have no doubt that most of the instances cited in support of a narrow interpretation of the establishment clause are inconsistent with its spirit and intent."[30] Ironically, his concern for "spirit and intent" was contradicted by his own words just 27 pages earlier!

The Friedmans would not appear to be impressed by Pfeffer's argumentation: "We believe that the penalty that is now imposed on parents who do not send their children to public schools violates the spirit of the First Amendment, whatever lawyers and judges may decide about the letter."[31]

A wide range of opinion on the religion clauses of the First Amendment can be readily perceived.

Separation of Church and State

The "wall of separation between Church and State" had its origin in a letter of Thomas Jefferson to the Danbury Baptist Association in which he denied their petition for a national day of prayer and fasting.[32] Since the *Everson* case of 1947, this metaphor has played a major role in many cases relating to Church-State relations which have been brought to the Supreme Court. The position of "absolute separatists" is well known[33] and needs no further documentation or elucidation. There is, however, a group of scholars who analyze the "separation" doctrine differently and whose views have not as yet been sufficiently heard.

O'Neill has attempted to "second-guess" Jefferson:

> We know conclusively, if we know Jefferson,
> that he could not have been thinking of a wall so
> high, so impregnable, so absolute, so completely
> without gates, or stiles, or friendly openings, as
> forever to prohibit any intercourse, neighborly
> help, or cooperation of any kind between government
> and religion.[34]

What at first glance may appear as wishful thinking was affirmed by the *American Bar Association Journal* in a 1948 editorial: "As President of the United States, Jefferson

used public funds and government properties in aid of religion and religious education in various ways."[35] This was
precisely Senator Packwood's conclusion, cited earlier in
this chapter.

Hutchins has refused to deal with the concept at all:
"The wall has done what walls usually do: it has obscured
the view . . . the wall is offered as a reason. It is not a
reason; it is a figure of speech."[36] He went on to declare
that "the wall has no future because it cannot help us to
learn."[37] Abraham counseled against heavy reliance on this
image because "the doctrine of the 'wall' is no solution *per
se*. It fails because the necessary line depends overrid-
ingly on public policy considerations--and on the interests
of contending groups."[38]

Clancy has argued against the concept ˙from yet another
angle:

> The 'wall of separation' metaphor is an unfor-
> tunate and inexact description of the American
> Church-State situation. What we have constitu-
> tionally is not a 'wall' but a logical distinction
> between two orders of competence. . . . The 'wall'
> of separation between Church and State, as it
> is conceived by most 'absolute separatists' in
> America, is not really a constitutional concept.
> It is rather a private doctrine.[39]

Kurland wrote that the principle of separation "is
meant to provide a starting point for solutions to problems
brought before the Court, not a mechanical answer to them."[40]
Kauper advocated understanding this principle as derived
from the First Amendment and, consequently, dependent on it
for its meaning:

> The *Zorach* opinion recognizes that the First
> Amendment itself says nothing about the separation
> of Church and State. Separation is not in itself a
> starting point in constitutional thinking. It
> follows and is required only to the extent that it

flows from the clauses related to non-establishment and the free exercise of religion.[41]

Katz recalled the purpose of separation: "Separation ordinarily promotes religious freedom; it is defensible so long as it does so, and only so long."[42] In another work, he drew out an important implication of a policy of absolute separation: "A rule of absolute separation would mean outlawing provisions designed to implement religious freedom, as in the armed forces."[43] Using England as an example, Littell asserted that "religious liberty and a 'wall of separation' are not identical."[44]

Blanshard, an inveterate opponent of parochial school aid, conceded:

> Our country did not formally establish separation of Church and State in educational matters until the nineteenth century. . . . Until about 1825 the religious denominationalism of elementary schools was taken for granted by the majority of Americans. Most schools before 1825 were Protestant.[45]

The inconsistencies in the application of the separation doctrine moved Brickman to observe:

> When a principle, such as that of Church-State separation, has been consistently violated with common consent over the years, it is reasonable to inquire if it has not been downgraded to an 'un-principle' or 'anti-principle.'[46]

However, the expression "separation of Church and State" has taken on an air of unchangeable doctrine or immutable truth. Nevertheless, Marnell challenged the Supreme Court's reliance on this approach:

> It is one of the curious anomalies of the recent history of the Supreme Court that a Court whose membership has shown a vigorous readiness to apply new viewpoints to certain ancient problems of society should view the American relationship of

Church and State as if it has been from the beginning and was as the law of the Medes and the
Persians, which altereth not.[47]

No Establishment and Free Exercise in Conflict

If the constitutional provision forbidding an establishment of religion and the equally constitutional guarantee of
free exercise of religion conflict, which takes precedence?
Opinion is scattered, and the decisions of the Court have
varied. However, Byrnes's reading of history led him to
maintain that "when the two clauses conflict, the Free
Exercise Clause has generally been held to rule."[48] This
has occurred because, in Kauper's analysis, the Supreme
Court has "elevated religious liberty to the position of a
preferred freedom."[49] Tribe has asserted that:

> The free exercise principle should be dominant
> in any conflict with the anti-establishment prin-
> ciple. Such dominance is the natural result of
> tolerating religion as broadly as possible rather
> than thwarting at all costs even the faintest
> appearance of establishment.[50]

Many constitutional experts believe there is a direct
link between religious liberty in the context of the educational scene and government subsidy. Fritz-Nova declared:

> We might very well reason that there is an
> unreasonable interference with education if there
> is no assistance given for the nonpublic or sec-
> tarian schools. Very plausibly you might say
> there is a violation of the Fourteenth Amendment
> where certain types of parents and guardians are
> prevented from sending their children to private
> schools for various reasons.[51]

However, in *Norwood v. Harrison* the Supreme Court explicitly
rejected such a connection.

In speaking of a tax on stimulants, John Stuart Mill
contended that "every increase of cost is a prohibition to

those whose means do not come up to the augmented price; and
to those who do, it is a penalty laid on them for gratifying
a particular taste."[52] A clear analogy can be seen between
the situation described by Mill and the predicament of
parents desirous of a parochial school education for their
children. A philosophical justification for state aid can
be found in Maritain's position: "If education is not outside its [the State's] sphere, this function is to help
the family fulfill its mission, and to complement this
mission."[53] Logic of a like nature led Tribe to state that
the requirements of the free exercise clause of the First
Amendment "demand that government pursue the least drastic
means to a compelling secular end."[54]

Katz has argued that the government's position vis a
vis religion should be neutral. He saw this neutrality as
requiring state aid to parochial schools:

> While the government should not promote reli-
> gion, it not only may, but should, try to avoid
> restraining or burdening religious choices. And if
> groups wish to have parish schools, there seems to
> be a presumption in favor of so molding government
> fiscal policies as not to handicap that choice.[55]

Powell made an interesting suggestion as to why the
Supreme Court has had such difficulty in the parochial
school aid cases, when the free exercise clause appears as
such a ready solution. He perceived the heart of the matter
to lie in this area:

> [I]t [the Supreme Court] conceives free exercise of
> religion in such narrow terms, i.e., within the
> walls of the church or the home, it is not really
> cognizant of violations of the rights of others
> for which religion and education are much more
> intimately joined.[56]

While suggesting that state aid may be unconstitutional
since it would force the general populace to aid religion,

Pie raised an objection from the other side: "To insist that a man must spend his money to support an irreligious system of education, such as is contained in the public school system, is unfair."[57] The same logic was operative in Parsons's intriguing observation:

> No Catholic parent has yet sued to show that his religious liberty is violated by using his taxes exclusively for only one kind of school, a school to which his Church and religious conscience forbid him to send his children.[58]

Such thinking, however, is by no means universal. Archer remarked: "A devoutly religious parent, it seems to me, should be willing to sacrifice to insure that kind of education [parochial] for his or her children."[59] What about the poor? Isn't the right of religious liberty then restricted to the affluent? Archer responded, "I don't think so. . . . Where there's a will, there's a way."[60]

The entire argument has been dismissed by Gordon since he has seen tuition costs as a mere side effect of the prior choice of private education:

> But where the exercise of a valid function of government, such as the operation of a secular public school, does not bar the religious option of attendance at a church school and only *incidentally* imposes the costs of the exercise of that option, there has been no denial of freedom of religion. (emphasis added)[61]

Sobran's brilliant analysis of the situation is worthy of detailed consideration, especially since he links the establishment of religion question (in terms of church attendance) with the establishment of a unitary school system. His insights are not only logical but also novel:

> Let us spell out the analogy of this culture to an established church. When the state has an offi-cial religion, it may, as in England, tolerate others. But the established church is paid for out

of public monies taken compulsorily, as all taxes
are, from all citizens. You have to pay for it
whether you belong or not. If you want another
church in keeping with your own beliefs, you pay
for it out of the money the state has left you.
That is how our educational system now works:
you pay for the schools from which religion is
banned whether your children attend them or not,
whether you agree with them or not, whether you
think them good influences or not.[62]

It has become commonplace to assert that the rights of
the majority are as safe as the rights of any given minority. Swomley attacked Roman Catholics for being more
concerned with themselves than with the general public,
apparently rejecting the above axiom:

The weight of Roman Catholic thinking on elementary and secondary education seems more concerned with 'justice' or 'freedom of choice' for
Roman Catholics than with religious liberty for the
entire community."[63]

Tribe did not accept such thinking. On the contrary, he
said that "we must ask whether, in the present age, religious tolerance must cease to be simply a negative principle
and must become a positive commitment that encourages the
flourishing of conscience."[64]

Two Centuries of Living Under the First Amendment

Anyone who assumes that current bans on state aid to
nonpublic school parents are as old as the Constitution
would be in for a rude awakening by reading the history of
the question. Kraushaar put it rather bluntly: "Public
support for various types of denominational schools, as well
as religious instruction in the public common schools where
they existed, were the rule rather than the exception."[65]
Lachman further delineated the nature of the public schools
of New York when he described them as "Protestant sectarian

schools maintained by private association."[66] Kienel referred to these schools as "an extension of the Protestant Church. So much so that the Catholic Church established its own Catholic schools in protest to the 'Protestant' public schools."[67]

Religious control of schools was so much a fact of life that in 1889 Montana, the Dakotas, Wyoming and Washington had to adopt ordinances forbidding such control, in order to qualify for statehood.[68] O'Neill provided a list of state appropriations to religious schools, with the latest known date of such grants:

Maryland	1818
Pennsylvania	1838
New Hampshire	1845
New Jersey	1846
Indiana	1855
California	1870
New York	1871
Texas	1874
Mississippi	1878
New Mexico	1897[69]

It is important to note that the Fourteenth Amendment was passed in 1868--the amendment that the Supreme Court in *Lemon* said forbade the individual states, as well as the federal government, from providing substantial financial support to denominational schools.

Scanning the first century of the First Amendment's life brings out two facts:

1. Denominational schools received government support;

2. The public schools were effectively Protestant schools.

The reading of this century's experience of the religion clauses of the First Amendment would reveal a totally different story. The *Pierce* case followed the trajectory of earlier approaches to pluralism in education. According

to Drinan, the Court "recognized the right of the private
school to exist as a substitute for the public school,
thereby giving private schools a juridical status."[70]
Drinan's analysis continued in this way:

> *Everson* follows from *Pierce*. Public money, in
> other words, cannot logically be withheld from the
> private school if it is publicly accredited as an
> institution where children may fulfill their legal
> duty to attend school.[71]

Pfeffer picked up history where Drinan left off and
admitted, with dismay:

> When the *Everson* decision is coupled with
> the *Allen* decision they lead logically to the con-
> clusion that a State may, notwithstanding the First
> Amendment, finance practically every aspect of
> parochial education.

However, the *Allen* decision is followed in quick suc-
cession by nearly a dozen other cases, most of which had
disastrous consequences for nonpublic school parents. These
cases are summarized in Chapter V. Adamo offered one reason
for the decided change in attitude and mood in the Court,
perhaps simplistically but not fully unfounded: "Pfeffer
has been brilliantly successful in persuading the Supreme
Court that anything which is good for the Catholic Church
must be bad for the nation as a whole."[73] Rhodes has
reported that Mark DeWolfe Howe (a non-Catholic) had a
similar evaluation of the situation: "One day, in the
middle of taking up the then-current crop of church-state
cases . . ., he [Howe] said that what you think of all
these questions depends on what you think of the Catholic
Church."[74]

The confusion surrounding the constitutionality of this
issue is nothing less than astounding, so much so that Senator Packwood, during the tax credit debate, could proclaim:

There is a complete split in the authorities.
There is a split in the courts. For every constitutional expert the opponents of this bill can cite
saying it is unconstitutional, we can cite one
saying it is constitutional.[75]

Some members of the Senate used the doubtful state of
the question to argue that Congress had no right to enact
legislation of questionable constitutionality. Both Packwood
and Ribicoff denied the validity of that position.[76]
Moynihan went on to press the point:

But, however the Court does rule, the important
consideration is that its ruling will be accepted.
Nobody associated with this legislation intends
anything but the absolute acceptance of whatever
the court hands down. But given that acceptancy,
and pending any decision, we must not be expected
to yield up our own sense of historic reality, our
own disposition to state what we feel the outcome
ought to be.[77]

Tortora picked up on this line of reasoning but did not
exhibit a very hopeful attitude or outlook:

Similarly, the gathering support for tuition
tax credits may, in due course, founder on the
shoals of a Court decision that they violate the
'separation of church and state.' That such a
ruling would be a preposterous misreading of the
First Amendment's reference to 'establishment
of religion' doesn't give us any less reason to
predict it.   It would just represent (to para-
phrase Raoul Berger's indictment in *Government by
Judiciary*) 'another of the usurpations that bestrew
the path of the Court.'[78]

To determine if Tortora's criticism is valid, it is
necessary to look at the record of cases that the Supreme
Court has handled in regard to governmental assistance for
nonpublic school parents. The next chapter provides a summary of the legislation and the cases.

NOTES

CHAPTER IV

[1]"Current Comment," *America* 134 (13 March 1976): 193-4.

[2]Thomas O'Toole, ed., *Institute of Church and State* 2 (Villanova, Pa.: Villanova University School of Law, 1959), p. 65.

[3]*Ibid.*, pp. 40-1.

[4]333 U.S. 237 (1948).

[5]J. M. O'Neill, *Religion and Education under the Constitution* (New York: Harper & Bros., 1949), p. 11

[6]*The Debates and Proceedings in the Congress of the United States, 1789-1824* (Washington: 1834-1856), pp. 729-31.

[7]Thomas Emerson, et al., *Political and Civil Rights in the United States* (Boston: Little, Brown and Co., 1967), p. 29.

[8]William Miller, et al., *Religion and the Free Society* (New York: The Fund for the Republic, 1958), p. 49.

[9]Joseph Sobran, "The Abortion Culture," *The Human Life Review* 7 (Spring 1981): 19.

[10]95th Congress, p. 13202.

[11]Dumas Malone, *Jefferson and His Time: The Sage of Monticello* (Boston: Little, Brown & Co., 1981), p. 199.

[12]*Ibid.*, p. 270.

[13]Charles Black, *Structure and Relationship in Constitutional Law* (Baton Rouge: Louisiana State University Press, 1969), p. 13.

[14]Paul Kauper, *Religion and the Constitution* (Baton Rouge: Louisiana State University Press, 1964), p. 50.

[15]John Cogley, ed., *Religion in America* (New York: Meridian Books, 1958), p. 52.

[16]210 U.S. 81 (1908).

[17]Elwyn Smith, *Religious Liberty in the United States* (Philadelphia: Fortress Press, 1972), p. 252.

[18]Paul Freund, et al., *Constitutional Law: Cases and Other Problems* (Boston: Little, Brown & Co., 1967), p. 2098.

[19]Edward Corwin, *A Constitution of Powers in a Secular State* (Charlottesville, Va.: The Michie Co.), p. 61.

[20]Cogley, p. 102 *(supra, note 15)*.

[21]cf. *Cantwell v. Connecticut,* 310 U.S. 296 (1940).

[22]Wilber Katz, *Religion and American Constitutions* (Evanston, Ill.: Northwestern University Press, 1963), p. 30.

[23]Corwin, p. 114 *(supra, note 19)*.

[24]Katz, p. 66 *(supra, note 22)*.

[25]Dallin Oaks, ed., *The Wall between Church and State* (Chicago: University of Chicago Press, 1963), p. 62.

[26]Virgil Blum, *Freedom in Education* (Garden City, N.Y.: Doubleday, 1965), p. 100.

[27]Paul Kauper, *Civil Liberties and the Constitution* (Ann Arbor: University of Michigan Press, 1966), p. 18.

[28]374 U.S. 222 (1963).

[29]413 U.S. 823 (1973).

[30]Cogley, p. 79 *(supra, note 15)*.

[31]Milton & Rose Friedman, *Free to Choose* (New York: Avon Books, 1981), p. 154.

[32]Chester Antieau, et al., *Freedom from Federal Establishment* (Milwaukee: Bruce Publishing Co., 1964), p. 183.

[33]cf. The works of Blanshard, Pfeffer and Swomley cited in the References.

[34]O'Neill, p. 83 *(supra, note 5)*.

[35]"No Law but Our Own Prepossessions," *American Bar Association Journal,* June 1948, p. 484.

[36]Oaks, p. 19 *(supra,* note 25).

[37]*Ibid.,* p. 25.

[38]Henry Abraham, *Freedom and the Court* (New York: Oxford University Press, 1976), p. 252.

[39]Miller, pp. 27-28 *(supra,* note 8).

[40]Philip Kurland, *Religion and the Law* (Chicago: Aldine Publishing Co., 1962), p. 18.

[41]Kauper, p. 18 *(supra,* note 27).

[42]Cogley, p. 97 *(supra,* note 15).

[43]Katz, p. 13 *(supra,* note 22).

[44]Franklin Littell, *From State Church to Pluralism* (Garden City, N.Y.: Doubleday, 1962), p. 100.

[45]Paul Blanshard, *American Freedom and Catholic Power* (Boston: Beacon Press, 1960), p. 84.

[46]William Brickman, *Subsidized Pluralism in American Education* (New York: Society for the Advancement of Education, 1959), p. 115.

[47]William Marnell, *The First Amendment* (Garden City, N.Y.: Doubleday, 1966), p. 101.

[48]Lawrence Byrnes, *Religion and Public Education* (New York: Harper and Row, 1975), p. 64.

[49]Kauper, p. 43 *(supra,* note 27).

[50]Laurence Tribe, "Rights of Religious Autonomy," *American Constitutional Law* (Mineola, N.Y.: Foundation Press, 1978), p. 833.

[51]O'Toole, p. 94 *(supra,* note 2).

[52]John Stuart Mill, *On Liberty* (New York: Holt & Co., 1898), p. 178.

[53]Jacques Maritain, *The Rights of Man and Natural Law* (New York: Scribner's, 1947), p. 79.

[54]Tribe, p. 847 *(supra,* note 50).

[55]Katz, p. 77 *(supra,* note 22).

[56]James Powell, "Public Schools and the First Amendment," *America* 139 (1/8 July 1978): 8.

[57]O'Toole, p. 112 *(supra,* note 2).

[58]Wilfred Parsons, *The First Freedom* (New York: Declan McMullen Co., 1948), p. 121.

[59]Albert Menendez, "An Interview with Glen L. Archer," *Church and State* 29 (February 1976): 15.

[60]*Ibid.*

[61]Oaks, p. 89 *(supra,* note 25).

[62]Sobran, p. 12 *(supra,* note 9).

[63]John Swomley, *Religion, the State and the Schools* (New York: Pegasus Books, 1968), p. 48.

[64]Tribe, p. 834 *(supra,* note 50).

[65]Otto Krauschaar, *American Nonpublic Schools* (Baltimore: Johns Hopkins University Press, 1972), p. 20.

[66]George Kelly, ed., *Government Aid to Nonpublic Schools: Yes or No?* (New York: St. John's University Press, 1972), p. 22.

[67]Paul Kienel, *The Christian School* (Wheaton, Ill.: Victor Books, 1974), p. 71.

[68]Anson Stokes and Leo Pfeffer, *Church and State in the United States* (New York: Harper & Row, 1964), p. 435.

[69]O'Neill, p. 143 *(supra,* note 2).

[70]Oaks, p. 55 *(supra,* note 25).

[71]*Ibid.,* p. 60.

[72]Leo Pfeffer, *God, Caesar and the Constitution* (Boston: Beacon Press, 1975), p. 269.

[73]Salvatore Adamo, "Can Catholics, Jews Unite?" *National Catholic Reporter* 14 (27 January 1978): 11.

[74]Donald Kommers and Michael Wahoske, eds., *Freedom and Education* (Notre Dame; Notre Dame Law School Press, 1972), p. 48.

[75]95th Congress, p. 13310.

[76]*Ibid.,* p. 13194.

[77]*Ibid.,* p. 13196.

[78]Anthony Tortora, *"Ex Parte* McCardle," *National Review* 32 (19 September 1980): p. 1140.

CHAPTER V

LEGISLATIVE CONCERN FOR NONPUBLIC SCHOOL
PARENTS AND JUDICIAL RESPONSE: 1947-1980

From 1947 to the present, the Supreme Court of the United States has been embroiled in controversies on governmental aid to nonpublic school parents at an increasing rate. The time-lag between cases has narrowed from 20 years between the first two to the point where, in 1973, five cases were decided.

The state legislatures and the United States Congress have exhibited a genuine concern for nonpublic school students and have translated that concern into concrete programs. New Jersey, New York, Pennsylvania, Rhode Island and Ohio are the only states to have drafted extensive legislation for aid to nonpublic elementary and secondary students, and to have their legislation challenged in the Supreme Court, usually resulting in a loss of the most significant aid programs. It is no accident that these states also have the highest percentage of Roman Catholics in the nation, and hence, of Catholic schools as well.

This chapter contains a shorthand summary of the relevant cases, including a description of the challenged pieces of legislation.

Summary of Cases (1947-1980)

°*Everson v. Board of Education*, 330 U.S. 1 (1947).

A New Jersey statute authorized local school districts to make provision for the transportation of children "living

remote from any schoolhouse."[1] In accord with that statute,
Ewing Township provided bus transportation for children,
including those who attended private, parochial schools. A
taxpayer challenged the constitutionality of such payments
because of the denominational character of the schools in
question.

The Court, in a 5-4 decision, held that New Jersey's
statute was constitutional since the bus transportation was
part of a general program of health or welfare benefits for
all children in the State.

°*Flast v. Cohen,* 392 U.S. 83 (1968).

Titles I and II of the Elementary and Secondary Education Act of 1965 mandated the expenditure of federal funds
for educational services and materials for the benefit of
both public and private school children. Federal income
taxpayers opposing such expenditures sought a declaration of
unconstitutionality for the statute since religious schools
were included.

With five justices in the majority, three concurring,
and one dissent, the Court held that on questions relating to Congress's spending funds for purposes allegedly
violating the First Amendment's prohibition against an
establishment of religion, a federal taxpayer does have
standing to sue.

The decision did not rule on the constitutionality of
the challenged aid program; it merely affirmed the right of
the taxpayer to challenge an expenditure possibly violative
of the No Establishment Clause.

°*Board of Education v. Allen,* 392 U.S. 236 (1968).

Public school authorities in New York State were
required by a 1965 state law to lend secular textbooks free
of charge to public and private school students from grades

seven through twelve. A local school board, desirous of excluding parochial school children, challenged the constitutionality of the statute.

Five justices (with one other concurring) affirmed the constitutionality of the textbook loan, obviously accepting the legislative finding of the bill that this program sought "the correction of those imbalances in our education programs," and that such programs "are important to our national defense and the general welfare of the state."[2] Three justices dissented.

°*Walz v. Tax Commission*, 397 U.S. 664 (1970).

New York City provides tax exemptions for nonprofit religious, educational, or charitable organizations. A property owner maintained that the exemption forced him to contribute to religious institutions, and, on that basis, was unconstitutional.

In a six-justice majority opinion (with two concurring votes and one dissent), the Court held traditional tax exemptions for churches constitutional, especially in light of the long-standing historical sanction for such programs. Although not a school-related case, *Walz* obviously leads to the conclusion that the traditional tax exemptions of church-related schools are also constitutional. The Court, however, sharply distinguished between "subsidies" and "exemptions" for churches. *Walz*, therefore, does not control the question whether government may *positively* finance education in church-related schools.

°*Lemon v. Kurtzman, Earley v. DiCenso* ("Lemon I"), 403 U.S. 602 (1971).

The aid to denominational schools offered by Pennsylvania and Rhode Island programs was challenged in this case. Both state laws had as their stated goal the improvement of secular education in the nonpublic schools.[3]

The Pennsylvania law authorized the State to pay nonpublic schools for teachers' salaries, texts and instructional materials used for secular courses. In addition, the nonpublic schools had to maintain detailed accounting procedures and have their texts approved by the State. In a finding akin to that in the Rhode Island case, it was noted that Pennsylvania's nonpublic schools served 20% of the State's students, with 95% of them in Roman Catholic institutions.

Under the Rhode Island law teachers' salaries were to be supplemented up to 15%, provided that salary did not exceed the maximum paid to public school teachers. The teachers so aided had to be certified, to be employed in a nonpublic school in which the per-pupil expenditure was less than the average in the public schools, to teach only secular courses and use only instructional materials used in public schools. Additional findings included the facts that nonpublic schools in Rhode Island served approximately 25% of the student population, and that 95% of those schools were under Roman Catholic auspices.

The decision (majority of five, three concurring, one dissenting) held that the programs in question were unconstitutional because they created an excessive entanglement between government and religion, especially in view of the monitoring required to insure the State's secular objectives. Substantial support of religion was also brought forth as a consideration in the decision, although the Court declined to rule on this aspect of the question.

°*Tilton v. Richardson,* 403 U.S. 672 (1971).

A federal Act authorized grants to institutions of higher education for the construction of academic buildings, excluding those to be used for religious purposes. The Act further permitted unlimited use of the buildings to the colleges after 20 years. Taxpayers and residents of Connecticut instituted action against federal officials and sectarian colleges in the State.

Upon hearing this case brought to it for alleged violations of the First Amendment's establishment clause, the Court decided (5-4) that the construction grants were constitutional. The justices, however, were unable to agree on an opinion. In an 8-1 decision, the Court held the 20-year limit unconstitutional since it would provide substantial benefit to the religious institutions.

°*Lemon v. Kurtzman* ("Lemon II"), 411 U.S. 192 (1973).

This case was a sequel to *Lemon I,* which invalidated a Pennsylvania law contracting for services of parochial schools. In this case appellants opposed payment for services rendered for the period between the statute's enactment by the Legislature and its invalidation by the Court.

Four justices (with one concurring opinion and three dissents) ruled that the nonpublic schools could be reimbursed for secular services provided during that time period since the schools and the Pennsylvania Legislature had acted in good faith, presuming the statue's validity.

°*Levitt v. Committee for Public Education and Religious Liberty,* 413 U.S. 472 (1973).

A New York statute authorized the Legislature to fund various state-mandated services in nonpublic schools, both state-prepared and teacher-prepared. The per-pupil expenditures had no limitations expressed. The constitutionality of this law was challenged by a group of New York taxpayers.

In an 8-1 decision, the Court found such a program unconstitutional since spending was not limited to the secular functions of the nonpublic schools. It should be noted that the bill contained no statement of legislative findings or intent.

°*Cathedral Academy v. Committee for Public Education and Religious Liberty,* 412 U.S. 472 (1973).

New York State enacted legislation to reimburse non-public schools for expenses incurred in complying with state-mandated testing. In an 8-1 decision, the Court struck down the law as violative of the First Amendment because many of the tests were teacher-prepared and, in religious schools, the justices feared an impermissible mixing of the religious with the secular could result. They also reacted negatively to the fact that the State had not provided for any auditing procedures to insure that state funds could not be diverted to religious purposes.

°*Hunt v. McNair,* 413 U.S. 734 (1973).

South Carolina established an Authority to help institutions of higher education in the construction financing and refinancing of projects. Denominational colleges were included although a clause excepted religious facilities from the scope of the Act.

A 6-3 decision upheld the constitutionality of the program as falling within the limits defined by the Court in *Tilton v. Richardson.* The overriding considerations revolved around the lack of a pervasively sectarian atmosphere and a lack of ongoing state entanglement with religion.

°*Committee for Public Education and Religious Liberty v. Nyquist,* 413 U.S. 756 (1973).

New York funded three aid programs for nonpublic schools, based on a 1972 law.[4] The first was to assist with maintenance and repair operations; the second provided some tuition reimbursement for parents of nonpublic school children, while the third program established a state income tax adjustment for middle-income parents of nonpublic school pupils.

The Court, in a majority opinion subscribed to by six justices, disallowed all three programs of aid since they directly and substantially supported religious institutions, either by overt grants to the schools or by using parents as the conveyors of the monies.

The Court rendered this decision in spite of a finding of the Legislature that "the fiscal crisis in nonpublic education . . . caused a diminution of proper maintenance and repair programs, threatening the health, welfare and safety of nonpublic school children," especially in areas "identified by a high incidence of families receiving aid to dependent children and deteriorating physical structures." The bill had likewise explicitly limited the grants to expenditures which were "clearly secular, neutral and non-ideological in nature,"[5] a fact the Court expressly ignored in its opinion.

Three justices (Chief Justice Burger and Justices White and Rehnquist) voted to uphold the constitutionality of the income tax adjustment for parents.

°*Sloan v. Lemon,* 413 U.S. 825 (1973).

Following on the *Lemon I* decision, the Pennsylvania Legislature attempted to resolve the Court's concern over "excessive entanglement." Therefore, a law was enacted to provide some tuition relief for parents of nonpublic school students. The bill contained findings that nonpublic school parents "assist the state in reducing the rising costs of public education;" that "the immense impact of inflation, plus sharply rising costs of education," jeopardize parents' "constitutional right to choose nonpublic education for their children." Finally, the Legislature alluded to the "enormous added financial, educational and administrative burden" that would result if "any substantial number" of non-public school children transferred to the public sector.[6]

In a 7-2 decision, the Supreme Court struck down the legislation as violative of the Establishment Clause of the First Amendment because the Court refused to see the parents as anything but mere conduits of the funds destined for parochial schools.

°*Wheeler v. Barrera,* 417 U.S. 402 (1974).

Title I of the Elementary and Secondary Education Act called for the participation of private school students, as well as public, on a level that is "comparable". The State of Missouri refused to provide Title I teachers to parochial schools during regular school hours, although some other services and materials were provided. Parents of nonpublic school students argued that state policies had the illegal effect of denying their children "comparable" services.

The Supreme Court, in a five-man decision (with three concurring and one dissenting opinion), maintained that the federal requirement for "comparable" services did not necessitate the same services and that individual states could formulate alternate programs, so as not to violate state laws.

°*Meek v. Pittenger,* 421 U.S. 349 (1975).

Pennsylvania enacted legislation enabling nonpublic school children to receive auxiliary services (such as counseling and testing), texts and instructional materials already given to public school students, "on an equal basis."[7]

In an evenly split decision, the Court declared text loans constitutional but invalidated the other programs since both personnel and materials could be diverted to serve the sectarian mission of the religiously affiliated schools.

°*Roemer v. Board of Public Works,* 426 U.S. 736 (1976).

The Maryland Legislature authorized state aid to private colleges (excluding those which awarded only seminary or theology degrees), based on student enrollment figures. More than two-thirds of the colleges involved in the aid program were not under religious auspices. Provision was also made for state monies to be kept in a separate account and to keep records of expenditures, for state review.

The Court ruled (with three dissents) that private institutions of higher education whose students are not primarily engaged in theological studies are eligible for funds to be spent on secular programs, provided that a reporting system is established.

°*Wolman v. Walter,* 433 U.S. 229 (1977).

An Ohio Law[8] authorized the following benefits for non-public school students: (1) secular texts, (2) standardized testing and diagnostic services, (3) therapeutic work on-site, (4) remedial services administered by public school personnel at religiously neutral sites, (5) instructional materials and equipment comparable to those used in public schools, and (6) transportation and other services for field trips.

In a 6-3 decision, the Court held that the first four programs were constitutional. The Court also held, 6-3 (but with a different alignment of the justices), that the last two programs were unconstitutional. The majority held that the involvement of parochial school personnel in the last program could add sectarian coloration to an apparently neutral field trip.

°Committee for Public Education and Religious Liberty v. Regan, 444 U.S. 646 (1980).

A New York statute directed payment to nonpublic schools for costs incurred in their complying with state-mandated requirements, such as testing, reporting and record-keeping. The statute also provided for auditing of the state funds, to insure that the monies were used only for the secular purposes intended by the Legislature, purposes which they perceived as "a matter of state duty and concern,"[9] and hence legitimate objects of state support.

In a 5-4 decision, the Supreme Court found that the statute does not violate the Establishment Clause of the First Amendment since the legislation had a legitimate secular goal, namely, the facilitating of a quality education for all children in New York State. It did not hold as of consequence that some of the tests were graded by nonpublic school personnel; nor did it find that the auditing procedures involved the State with excessive entanglement, or that the primary effect of the statute was religious rather than secular.

Conclusion

This thumbnail sketch of the relevant cases should indicate the scope of the matter, as well as the difficulty in ascertaining a definite direction in which the Court has moved. Throughout the last decade, a majority of the Court has sustained the constitutionality of such "ancillary" public assistance as transportation, textbooks, school lunches, health services and standardized testing. A more detailed analysis of the opinions of the Court and the influences on those opinions would be instructive and needed to obtain a more nuanced understanding of the matter at hand.

NOTES

CHAPTER V

[1]"Transportation of Children Remote from School," N.J.R.S. Cum. Supp., Tit. 18, c. 14, § 8.

[2]Power to Designate Textbooks; Purchase and Loan of Textbooks; Purchase of Supplies," New York Sess. Laws 1965, c. 320, § 1.

[3]"Nonpublic Elementary and Secondary Education Act," Pa. Laws, Tit. 24, § 5601, Repealed.
"Legislative Findings—Declaration of Policy," General Laws of Rhode Island, § 16-51-1, Repealed.

[4]"Health and Safety Grants for Nonpublic School Children," N.Y. Laws 1972, c. 414, § 1, amending N.Y. Education Law, Art. 12, §§ 549-553 (Supp. 1972-1973).

[5]*Ibid.*

[6]"Parent Reimbursement Act for Nonpublic Education," Pa. Laws 1971, Act 92, Pa. Stat. Ann., Tit. 24, §§ 5701 et seq. (Supp. 1973-1974).

[7]"Auxiliary Services," Act 194, § 1 (a), Pa. Stat. Ann., Tit. 24, § 9-972 (a); Act 195, § 1 (a), Pa. Stat. Ann., Tit. 24, § 9-972 (a).

[8]"Distribution of Payments for Special Programs," Ohio Rev. Code Ann. § 3317.06 (Supp. 1976).

[9]"Apportionment of State Monies to Nonpublic Schools," N.Y. Laws 1974, ch. 507, as amended by ch. 508.

CHAPTER VI

THE SUPREME COURT'S STEREOTYPE
OF THE PAROCHIAL SCHOOL

Stereotyping is a dangerous activity, especially for those stereotyped.[1] Throughout history various groups have fallen victim to the technique; unfortunately, stereotypes die hard, and hence many unthinking people still regard Italians as crime-connected, blacks as shiftless, Jews as grasping, Irish as alcoholic, women as mindless and Poles as ignorant--even though such generalizations have been disproved time and again. The popular imagination, however, has been impressed by the repetition of the charges and the long-standing nature of the claims.

It is a major contention of this work that Catholic schools have been unfairly stereotyped, and that the persistence of the stereotype, especially in the minds of many members of the Supreme Court, is a principal cause of repeated denials by the Court of programs to aid parochial school parents. It is a further contention that the Court has traditionally relied for information on sources inimical to Catholic interests.

There seems to be a direct connection between how the respective justices view the parochial school and whether or not they vote to permit the aid program in question to stand.[2] That in itself is a serious difficulty, but one must also remember that there exists no monolithic pattern for "the parochial school," varying as the schools do not only from diocese to diocese, but even from parish to

parish.   This second point is dealt with extensively in
Chapter VII.

It is also important to note at the outset that although
many denominations operate educational institutions, the
Supreme Court has chosen to speak only of Catholic schools
in delineating qualities or characteristics of a dominant
profile, except in the college cases.   It is also important
at this point to consider how a judge comes to a particular
position, which then becomes the law of the land.

The Myths and the Reality of the Judicial Process

The average citizen tends to view the judicial process
as dispassionate and aloof from every day biases.   This is
to forget that a judge is a person with the same human
foibles and prejudices as the rest of humanity.   It was
precisely this realization that led Sorauf to observe how
important it is to "look for hints and clues in the judge's
personal life--his own religious background and affiliation
if the issue is church-state relations--and in his written
opinions, his offhand utterances, and his general judicial
demeanor. . . ."[3]   He further noted that the parochial
school aid issue seems to "trigger" something in state trial
court judges, who are Protestant, from a normally moderate
position on Church-State separation into an absolutist
position.[4]

Similar tendencies in the Supreme Court have caused
people like Morgan to express concern: "It is fair to say
of the majority of the Warren Court that in the free exercise area a diffuse desire to protect unorthodox minorities
led it, helter-skelter, into a major doctrinal innovation."[5]
Nagel remarked in a like vein in reference to the Burger
Court, stating that its reputation "within the legal pro-

fession is miserable [because of] a basic uncertainty as to what the Constitution means."[6]

In testifying before the Senate Judiciary Committee on the proposed Human Life Bill, Bork of Yale Law School expressed his opinion that *Roe v. Wade* was "an unconstitutional decision, a serious and wholly unjustifiable judicial usurpation of State legislative authority." He went on to declare that he believed that decision was "by no means the only example of such unconstitutional behavior by the Supreme Court."[7]

The Founding Fathers warned of such developments and even got glimpses of these developments while the nation was in its embryonic stages. Hamilton asserted that if judges "should be disposed to exercise Will instead of Judgement, the consequence would . . . be the substitution of their pleasure to that of the legislative body."[8] The specter of the Court consistently at loggerheads with the will of Congress was given short shrift by Jefferson in a letter to Abigail Adams:

> But the opinion which gives to the judges the right to decide what laws are constitutional and what not, not only for themselves in their own sphere of action, but for the legislature and executive also, in their spheres would make the judiciary a despotic branch.[9]

Jefferson's worst fears must have been realized in his own day for he commented that "our Judges are effectually independent of the nation. But this ought not to be." He further alleged that he saw a pattern emerging whereby they attempt to gain "further hold for future advances of power."[10]

The present discussion could be considered as unduly biased against the judges were only characters from history to speak, or those upset by Supreme Court decisions. Justice

William O. Douglas himself admitted in his autobiography how unscientific the work of the Court is. He recalled a session with Chief Justice Charles Evans Hughes in which Douglas, as the junior justice, was being advised by the eldest. Hughes counseled: "Justice Douglas, you must remember one thing. At the constitutional level where we work, ninety percent of any decision is emotional. The rational part of us supplies the reasons for supporting our predilections."[11]

A *National Review* commentary took on new meaning in the light of Hughes's statement. The writers spoke of the need to evaluate the decisions of the Court in a very broad context, for:

> [T]aken purely in constitutional terms, many
> Supreme Court decisions during the present era seem
> the products of spontaneous generation. Under-
> stood as rooted in concrete political and economic
> interests, they become more intelligible.[12]

The Court itself has tried to project and maintain the image of men untouched by any interests beyond the constitutional:

> In determining whether a law violates the pro-
> visions of the First Amendment concerning religion,
> the constitutional standard is the separateness of
> church and state, and not the individual prefer-
> ences of the members of the Supreme Court.[13]

However, even official documents let slip an occasional hint of subjectivity, like this most famous one: "It is a matter in which we can find no law but our own prepossessions."[14] Or, as the eminent jurist, Benjamin Cardozo, noted: "The great tides and currents which engulf the rest of men do not turn aside in their course, and pass the judges by."[15]

The Cases

Is it possible that personal "predilections", to use Chief Justice Hughes's word, play a significant part in Supreme Court decisions on the constitutionality of various aid programs to benefit parochial school children? Is a justice's decision dependent on how he perceives or feels about parochial schools? Hypotheses such as these can be tested only by a careful reading of the cases, to which attention is now returned.

1. *Everson*, 330 U.S. 1 (1947).

Justice Hugo Black, in delivering the opinion of the Court on this parochial school busing case, reflected on parochial schools and their constituencies' rights in this rather objective way:

> These church schools give their students, in addition to secular education, regular religious instruction conforming to the religious tenets and modes of worship of the Catholic faith. The superintendent of these schools is a Catholic priest. (at 3)
> We cannot say that the First Amendment pro-hibits New Jersey from spending tax-raised funds to pay the bus fares of parochial school pupils as a part of a general program under which it pays the fares of pupils attending public and other schools. It is undoubtedly true that children are helped to get to church schools. (at 17)
> . . . cutting off church schools from these services [police and fire protection], so separate and so indisputably marked off from the religious function, would make it far more difficult for the schools to operate. But such is obviously not the intention of the First Amendment. (at 18.)

The majority opinion, then, acknowledged the existence of religious influences, but did not reflect on them in a negative manner. Furthermore, Black did not believe the Constitution required him to do so. New Jersey's busing of parochial school students was thus upheld.

The dissent of Justice Jackson, however, revealed a far different attitude toward parochial schools:

> I have a sympathy, though it is not ideological, with Catholic citizens who are compelled by law to pay taxes for public schools, and also feel constrained by conscience and discipline to support other schools for their own children. (at 18)
> But we know that such schools are parochial only in name--they, in fact, represent a world-wide and age-old policy of the Roman Catholic Church. . . . It relies on early and indelible indoctrination in the faith and order of the Church by word and example of persons consecrated to the task. (footnote at 22f)
> Our public school, if not a product of Protestantism, is at least more consistent with it than with the Catholic culture and scheme of values. I would not be surprised if any Catholic would deny that the parochial school is a vital, if not the most vital, part of the Roman Catholic Church. . . . Catholic education is the rock on which the whole structure rests, and to render tax aid to its Church schools is indistinguishable to me from rendering the same aid to the Church itself. (at 24)
> The policy of our Federal Constitution has never been pleasing to most religious groups. They all are quick to invoke its protections; but all are irked when they feel its restrictions. (at 27)

Justice John Rutledge's dissent from the majority opinion ran along the lines of thought akin to Jackson's:

> It [bus transportation] aids them in a substantial way to get the very thing which they are sent to the particular school to secure, namely, religious training and teaching. (at 45)
> There is undeniably an admixture of religious with secular teaching in all such institutions. (at 47)
> The child attending the religious school has the same right as any other to attend the public school. But he foregoes exercising it. . . . (at 58)
> Like St. Paul's freedom, religious liberty with a great price must be bought. And for those who exercise it most fully, by insisting upon religious education for their children mixed with secular, by

the terms of our Constitution the price is greater than for others.   (at 59)

Echoes of Jackson's philosophy of parochial education can be heard in Conant's remarks:

> The greater the proportion of our youth who fail to attend our public schools and who receive their education elsewhere, the greater the threat to our democratic unity.   To use taxpayers' money to assist private schools is to suggest that American society use its own hands to destroy itself.[16]

The only difference is in style, rather than in content, it would seem.

How little of the content of the dissenting justices' opinions was original with them can be seen by a comparison with the similar points gleaned from the brief filed by the American Civil Liberties Union against the busing legislation for parochial school students:

> There can be no question that parochial schools generally and Catholic parochial schools in particular are private, religious, sectarian schools and institutions.   They are not public schools or part of the public school system.   It is recognized that parochial schools are instituted by the Catholic Church so that the youth thereof may receive instruction in its religious principles and beliefs along with secular education.   Systematic religious instruction and moral training according to the tenets of that Church are regularly provided.   The schools are supported and maintained by the local church parish and diocese.   Invariably, the teachers are members of an order.   Religious worship, as well as religious instruction, is involved.   That secular subjects are also taught there does not change their character.[17]

The majority of the Court rejected this one-sided, negative image of Catholic schools; the legislation passed muster.   However, if the dissenting justices who had accepted the ACLU brief as valid had convinced one more justice of the validity of those and similar claims, the bill would have been declared unconstitutional.

2. *Flast,* 392 U.S. 83 (1968).

Although not a parochial school aid case *per se,* in a concurring opinion which would grant standing to a taxpayer to challenge possible governmental assistance in violation of the First Amendment, Justice William Douglas demonstrated his feelings toward proponents of state aid to parochial schools by the loaded language he used: "The mounting federal aid to sectarian schools is notorious and the subterfuges numerous." (at 113)

The justice seemed to ignore the fact that the same could have been said of any group in history that has advocated unpopular legislation: abolitionists, suffragettes, civil rights activists. It is unfortunate that a Supreme Court justice would need to be reminded that simply because he does not like a proposed bill that such efforts cannot *ipso facto* be characterized as "subterfuges," nor that the advocates can be denied their constitutional rights of freedom of speech and freedom to petition the government for a redress of grievance.

3. *Allen,* 392 U.S. 236 (1968).

Justice White wrote the opinion of the Court on this textbook loan case. It included the following statements:

> . . . [T]his Court has long recognized that religious schools pursue two goals, religious instruction and secular education. (at 245)
> . . . [W]e cannot agree with appellants either that all teaching in a sectarian school is religious or that the processes of secular and religious training are so intertwined that secular textbooks furnished to students by the public are in fact instrumental in the teaching of religion. (at 248)

Dissenting from the majority opinion (and accepting the allegations of the appellants),[18] Justice Black reflected a most negative attitude toward those seeking governmental assistance for parochial schools:

> The same powerful sectarian religious propagandists who have succeeded in securing passage of the present law to help religious schools carry on their sectarian religious purposes can and doubtless will continue their propaganda, looking toward complete domination and supremacy of their particular brand of religion. (at 252)
> The First Amendment's prohibition against governmental establishment of religion was written on the assumption that state aid to religion and religious schools generates discord, disharmony, hatred, and strife among our people, and that any government that supplies such aid is to that extent a tyranny. (at 254)

This surely appears to be a different Justice Black from the man who wrote the rather favorable remarks recorded above in *Everson*.

A powerful distrust of parochial school teachers and administrators came across in Justice Douglas's dissent:

> This initial and crucial selection [of books] is undoubtedly made by the parochial school's principal or its individual instructors, who are, in the case of Roman Catholic schools, normally priests and nuns. (at 255)
> Can there be the slightest doubt that the head of the parochial school will select the book or books that best promote its sectarian creed? (at 256)

Douglas also expressed concern that Catholic editions of secular texts might be used and that "the religious endorsements could easily be removed by the author and publisher at the next printing" (footnote at 259). In pursuing this vignette of parochial school manipulation of statutes to their benefit and the theme of religious permeation of the total curriculum, Douglas referred to the entire process as "creeping sectarianism". (footnote at 260) No doubt, Douglas found merit in the appellants' claim that: "There is no such thing as secular education in a sectarian elementary or secondary school. The whole curriculum is permeated by religion."[19]

In a dissent similar to Douglas's, Justice Abe Fortas chose to ignore the fact that the law in question stipulated that text selection was limited to books that could be used in a public school, as well as the fact that texts differ from district to district even within the state system of schools, dependent upon the preferences of faculty and administration. He asserted the following:

> Public funds are used to buy, for students in sectarian schools, textbooks which are selected and prescribed by the sectarian schools themselves. (at 269)
> But this program is not one in which all children are treated alike, regardless of where they go to school.
> This program, in its unconstitutional features, is handtailored to satisfy the specific needs of sectarian schools. Children attending such schools are given *special* books--books selected by the sectarian authorities. (at 271)

Once again it appears that the constitutional arguments had little to do with the outcome of the decision. Most of the opinions centered on the profile of the Catholic school, as the several justices perceived it. Some were extremely concerned about the identity and religious affiliation of parochial school personnel. The majority had a positive impression of school and faculty and permitted the aid program to continue. The dissenting justices were convinced otherwise and voted to discontinue the plan.

4. *Lemon I*, 403 U.S. 602 (1971).

In this case dealing with state subsidy of parochial school teacher's salaries, the opinion of the court was

delivered by Justice Warren Burger. The image of the
parochial school that the justices painted emerged thus:
". . . church-related elementary and secondary schools have
a significant religious mission . . . a substantial portion
of their activities are religiously oriented." (at 613)
Burger went on to sketch out what he deemed to be salient
indicators of the religious nature of Catholic schools.
They are "located close to parish churches;" "identifying
religious symbols" are in evidence. Even though "only
approximately 30 minutes a day are devoted to direct religious instruction, there are religiously oriented extra-
curricular activities." He went on to note that two-thirds
of the teachers were nuns whose "dedicated efforts provide
an atmosphere in which religious instructions and religious
vocations are natural and proper parts of life in such
schools." He asserted that the various elements of the
schools make them "a powerful vehicle for transmitting the
Catholic faith to the next generation." Burger's strong
objection seemed to revolve around the issue of "the
impressionable age of the pupils." (at 615-6)

The majority opinion then proceeded to discuss the
question of the faculties of Catholic schools, maintaining
"that teachers have a substantially different ideological
character from books" because "a text book's content is
ascertainable, but a teacher's handling of a subject is
not." This was especially troublesome to the majority
because the teachers in question were "under religious
control and discipline." (at 617)

That "religious authority necessarily pervades the
school system" was sufficiently obvious to the majority
justices because administrative decisions were made by the
bishop, priests and nuns. (at 617)

Even though the District Court found that teachers of secular subjects did not necessarily bring in religion, the majority opinion held that "what has been recounted suggests the potential if not actual hazards of this form of state aid." And that was enough. They explained their position thus:

> We need not and do not assume that teachers in parochial schools will be guilty of bad faith or any conscious design to evade the limitations imposed by the statute and the First Amendment. We simply recognize that a dedicated religious person, teaching in a school affiliated with his or her faith and operated to inculcate its tenets, will inevitably experience great difficulty in remaining religiously neutral . . . (at 618-9)

The final concern expressed by the majority was the element of political divisiveness brought on by on-going discussions on the topic of governmental assistance to non-public school parents:

> In a community where such large numbers of pupils are served by church-related schools, it can be assumed that state assistance will entail considerable political activity. Partisans of parochial schools, understandably concerned with rising costs and sincerely dedicated to both the religious and secular educational missions of their schools, will inevitably champion this cause and promote political action to achieve their goals. . . . To have States or communities divide on the issues presented by state aid to parochial schools would tend to confuse and obscure other issues of great urgency. (at 622-3).

Carried to its logical conclusion, this doctrine would effectively disenfranchise religiously motivated people from participation in the process of a special interest group society. If invoked earlier, it would have meant clergy could not have spoken out on behalf of civil rights; at present it would also mean that Jews could not seek aid for

Israel since this is a sensitive, divisive issue which could "confuse and obscure issues of great urgency."

The composite picture was one painted in broad strokes so strong that one could legitimately wonder when secular instruction could ever occur. The indicia of religiosity were first catalogued by LaNoue for *Phi Delta Kappan* in June 1962, and quoted by Clausen in his brief in this case for United Americans for Public Schools.[20] All of LaNoue's criteria found complete acceptance by the majority of the Court. It should be noted that this is the same Clausen who has just published a tract in defense of public education, but the overall impact of which is to present the Roman Catholic Church as an enemy of freedom, the American way, and the U.S. Constitution, most notably in his treatments of "The Vatican Problem" and "Religion at War," complete with pictures of instruments of torture from the Spanish Inquisition.[21]

Parochial school teachers were portrayed as untrustworthy, and parents concerned about their children's education were labeled partisan. The entire description was one of damning with faint praise, and the pattern reached a crescendo in the concluding statement of the opinion: "Nothing we have said can be construed to disparage the role of church-related elementary and secondary schools in our national life."

Douglas was joined by Black in a concurring opinion which continued the pattern, but in highly charged language:

> The zeal of religious proselytizers promises to carry the day and make a shambles of the Establishment Clause. Moreover, when taxpayers of many faiths are required to contribute money for the propagation of one faith, the Free Exercise Clause is infringed. (at 627-8)

Furthermore, parochial schools were described as promoting "individual idiosyncracies" (at 630), resulting in the "problem of policing sectarian schools." (at 631) "The curriculum presents subtle and difficult problems" (at 634), due no doubt to the presence of the kind of teacher described as a "religious zealot". (at 635)

The question of permeation came to the fore again in the following statements made by Douglas:

> Sectarian education, however, does not remedy that condition. The advantages of sectarian educa-tion relate solely to religious or doctrinal mat-ters. They give the church the opportunity to indoctrinate its creed delicately and indirectly, or massively through doctrinal courses. (at 630-1)
> Sectarian instruction, in which, of course, a State may not indulge, can take place in a course on Shakespeare or in one on mathematics. No matter what the curriculum offers, the question is, what is *taught?* We deal not with evil teachers but with zealous ones who may use any opportunity to indoctrinate a class. (at 635)

As proof for the above, Douglas quoted from a 1958 work of a Jesuit priest, as though that still represented the Catholic approach to education and also as though the Second Vatican Council had never happened between 1958 and 1971.

Needless to say, Douglas did not come up with that source on his own. The *amicus* brief of the American Jewish Committee, et al., cited Father Fichter's book as "author-itative" for Catholic education, and particularly on the matter of religious permeation of the curriculum. The brief argued that this permeation "leaves no place for purely secular instruction in the Catholic school; indeed, the term 'secular education' is almost self-contradictory in such schools." The document went on to speak about the situation in the language of human reproduction: "everything must be impregnated with God and religion."[22]

In addition to this quote from Fichter, Douglas referred
extensively to a work of Loraine Boettner which is nothing
short of anti-Catholic "hate" literature.[23] This work was
intended to corroborate Douglas's impressions of the nature
and purpose of Catholic education!   Surely this is what
Fitzpatrick meant when he said: "If people who share
Loraine Boettner's opinion of Catholicism are influencing
the Supreme Court, the future for American Catholics could
be very bleak indeed."[24]   Senator Moynihan took serious
exception to this citation on the Senate floor during
the congressional debate on tax credits and used it as
an illustration of the kind of blatant and unrefuted anti-
Catholicism that is countenanced in otherwise civil
circles.[25]

He then quoted with approval from a statement of the
Justice William Brennan's opinion took a slightly different tack as he concentrated on parochial vs. public
education: "This nation long ago committed itself to primary reliance upon publicly supported public education to
serve its important goals in secular education." (at 658)

He then quoted with approval from a statement of the
Court in the *Schempp* case:

> It is implicit in the history and character of
> American public education that the public schools
> serve a uniquely *public* function: The training of
> American citizens in an atmosphere free of paro-
> chial, divisive, or separatist influences of any
> sort--an atmosphere in which children may assimi-
> late a heritage common to all American groups and
> religions. (at 658)

Nor did this pitting of public schools against parochial
schools originate with Brennan.   It came from Pfeffer's
brief, filed on behalf of the American Association of
School Administrators, who saw the statute in question as
"siphon[ing] off public funds for nonpublic schools."   It
warned that, "unless halted, the inevitable result will be a

proliferation of private schools with an escalation of the exodus of middle class children from public schools."[26]

Brennan's and Pfeffer's statements can hardly be distinguished from that of Blanshard:

> There are a great many communities in which the Catholic schools drain off from the public schools at least one-quarter of the community's children. . . . The separation is particularly harmful when . . . the Catholic group is largely an immigrant group that needs assimilation and Americanization more than any other part of the community.[27]

Justice White's dissent was written in a spirit that would let the record speak for itself, presuming good-will and professionalism on the part of parochial school teachers:

> The reasoning [of the majority] is a curious and mystifying blend, but a critical factor appears to be an unwillingness to accept the District Court's express findings that on the evidence before it none of the teachers here involved mixed religious and secular instruction. (at 666)
>
> Although stopping short of calling them [parochial school teachers] untrustworthy, the Court concludes that for them the difficulties of avoiding teaching religion along with secular subjects would pose intolerable risks and would in any event entail an unacceptable enforcement regime. (at 666)
>
> The Court points to nothing in the record indicating that any participating teacher had inserted religion into his secular teaching or had had any difficulty in avoiding doing so. (at 667)

White concluded his dissent with what might be construed as a strong rebuke to the majority in the case: "I would no more here than in the Rhode Island case substitute presumption for proof that religion is or would be taught in state-financed secular courses." (at 670)

The end result was that once more parochial school parents had been denied aid because a majority of the justices relied on a hypothetical profile of their schools, a profile presented by less than objective sources, one in direct contradiction to the trial record's evidence, but a profile nonetheless accepted by the majority. Landynski saw the whole situation resulting from "underdeveloped reasoning and overdeveloped imagination which when discovered in the views held by right-wing politicians, liberals loudly deplore."[28]

5. *Tilton*, 403 U.S. 672 (1971).

Chief Justice Warren Burger delivered the opinion of the Court, which permitted religious colleges to receive government grants for building projects. Throughout the majority opinion, an effort was made to justify this action by contrasting parochial education at the college level with its counterparts at the elementary and secondary levels. Some examples follow:

> There [in Allen] the Court refused to assume that religiosity in parochial elementary and secondary schools necessarily permeates the secular education that they provide. This record, similarly, provides no basis for any such assumption here. (at 681)

This finding was all the more remarkable because just pages earlier, they did assert that permeation was a very real problem. They went on to indicate that "we cannot, however, strike down an Act of Congress on the basis of a hypothetical 'profile'." (at 682) Nevertheless, state statutes for lower education were struck down "on the basis of a hypothetical 'profile'." Appellees in the case argued successfully that "appellants' so-called 'composite profile' of a 'sectarian' college is a stereotype that exists only in appellants' fertile imagination."[29] The appellees proceeded to condemn the appellants' attempts "to create a rule of constitutional law in a factual vacuum." Rather, they asserted, "a decision should be firmly rooted in a factual record developed through the adversary process and not on the basis of stereotypes and composite profiles which, for all the Court knows, exist only in the mind of the appellants."[30]

Appellees obviously convinced the majority of the Court for they declared that the building of a language laboratory was obviously "to assist students with their pronunciation in modern foreign languages--a use which would seem peculiarly unrelated and unadaptable to religious indoctrination." (at 681)

The opinion went on to assert that "there is substance to the contention that college students are less impressionable and less susceptible to religious indoctrination." (at 686) However, that dictum was never substantiated in any way. Senator Moynihan attacked this very same assertion in the tax credit debate of the 95th Congress from logic[31] and from science[32] when it came from the Attorney General. Even Pfeffer has found the higher vs. lower education distinction insupportable.[33]

The final conclusion, however, was quite simple and forthright: "In short, the evidence shows institutions with admittedly religious functions but whose predominant higher education mission is to provide their students with a secular education."

Acceptance by the Court of a positive image of religiously oriented education (that is, religious and secular education which are separate) resulted in the Court's upholding of the congressional legislation.

6. *Lemon II,* 411 U.S. 192 (1973).

The only new statement to appear in this "follow-up" case was what might be considered an interesting admission of the Court. They held that reimbursements could be made to parochial schools officials because "state officials and those with whom they deal are entitled to rely on a presumptively valid state statute, enacted in good faith and by no means plainly unlawful." (at 209)

This was precisely the point made by appellees in the case as they argued in their brief that they:

> . . . cannot let go unchallenged their [appellants'] erroneous and irresponsible high-sounding appeal to public policy . . ., where they charge the Legislature of Pennsylvania and indirectly those who seek and support aid to nonpublic education--with conduct tantamount to conspiracy, legislative fraud and abuse of judicial process.[34]

The critical words of the Court, of course, were the last quoted: "enacted in good faith and by no means plainly unlawful."

7. *Levitt,* 413 U.S. 472 (1973).

Chief Justice Warren Burger once more delivered the opinion of the Court involved with funding to parochial schools for state-mandated services. The only statement that would add a new dimension to the parochial school profile compiled to date was the following:

> Yet, despite the obviously integral role of such testing in the total teaching process, no attempt is made under the statute, and no means are available, to assure that internally prepared tests are free of religious instruction. We cannot ignore the substantial risk that these examinations, prepared by teachers under the authority of religious institutions, will be drafted with an eye, unconsciously or otherwise, to inculcate students in the religious precepts of the sponsoring church. (at 480)

Burger's caution was directly traceable to the brief filed by Pfeffer for the appellees in this case, in which samples from teacher editions of texts offered questions and answers, suggesting ways to bring the religious dimension even into a mathematics class. Filers of the brief admitted that "we do not know if these books are still in use in any church schools, or if they are whether any teachers use the suggested tests and the suggested answers. But this we submit is constitutionally irrelevant. . . ."[35]

For the seventh time a majority of the Supreme Court had been swayed to accept a certain image of a parochial school and thereby to make a constitutional decision.

8. *Cathedral Academy*, 413 U.S. 472 (1973).

It is not necessary to dwell long on this case because a very similar one came before the Court seven years later. The reimbursements to the nonpublic schools, however, were declared unconstitutional because the majority of the justices were convinced that many of the tests used were problematic because they were teacher-prepared (rather than prepared by the State or other outside testing firm), that "no means are available . . . to assure that [they] . . . are free of religious instruction." (at 480)

This distrust of parochial school teachers had a long history, going back to the *Lemon* case, already discussed in detail. The LaNoue indicia of religiosity, which figured prominently there and in nearly every negative opinion of the Supreme Court justices since, likewise played a key role in the opinion of the majority in this case. (at 476) Needless to say, this hypothetical profile of the parochial school was hammered away at by Pfeffer in his brief for the appellees.[36] Having won the majority of the Court to his evaluation of parochial (especially Catholic) school teachers, the aid program was invalidated.

The State of New York remained committed to finding constitutionally acceptable ways of assisting nonpublic education. Hence the legislators of the State took the Court's opinion here, noted their objections to the present legislation, and tailored new legislation to meet their objections. This new attempt resulted in a bill challenged again by Pfeffer, this time as the *Regan* case of 1980.

9. *Hunt*, 413 U.S. 734 (1973).

In a decision based on the prior opinion of *Tilton*, Justice Powell spoke for the Court in upholding an aid program to benefit a Baptist college in South Carolina. The only finding to appear follows:

> What little there is in the record concerning the College establishes that there are no religious qualifications for faculty membership or student admission, and that only 60% of the College student body is Baptist, a percentage equivalent to the percentage of Baptists in that area of South Carolina. On the record in this case there is no basis to conclude that the College's operations are oriented significantly towards sectarian rather than secular education. (at 743-4)

10. *Nyquist*, 413 U.S. 756 (1973).

Among the statements offered in the majority opinion delivered by Justice Lewis Powell, one reads the following: "Although no record was developed in these cases a number of pertinent generalizations may be made about the nonpublic schools which would benefit from these enactments." (at 767) The Court went on to say that in all likelihood there might be deviations from the "generalizations", but they were sufficiently convinced that they held up so as to go on with their decision.

A major concern seemed to revolve around the potential for monies to be diverted to religious purposes:

> Nothing in the statute, for instance, bars a qualifying school from paying out of state funds the salaries of employees who maintain the school chapel, or the cost of renovating classrooms in which religion is taught, or the cost of heating and lighting these same facilities. Absent appro-

priate restrictions on expenditures for these and
similar purposes, it simply cannot be denied that
this section has a primary effect that advances
religion in that it subsidizes directly the religious activities of sectarian elementary and
secondary schools. (at 774)

The genesis and language of this argument of the Court came
from the appellants' brief:

> The argument is bottomed on the assumption that
> a parochial school budget is divisible. It rejects
> the argument that once a public subsidy is given it
> lightens the burden on the rest of the budget and
> even permits more of the other private money to be
> used for religious instruction. . . .
>   . . . No effort is made in this part of the
> statute to distinguish between secular and reli-
> gious education. The janitorial service embraces
> cleaning the chapel, where there is one, and heat
> is provided in the classrooms where religion is
> taught. There is no suggestion that heat is to be
> cut off while prayer or religious teaching is con-
> ducted in the same schoolrooms.[37]

The apparent pettiness and even snideness of the appellants did not deter the majority of the Court from advancing
the very points made in their brief. The image of ubiqui-
tous religion had seemingly reared its head, and that was
enough for unconstitutionality, in the opinion of the
majority.

White's dissent once again called for a reading of the
record and making that the basis of a decision:

> The Court's opinion emphasizes a particular
> kind of parochial school, one restricted to stu-
> dents of particular religious beliefs and condi-
> tioning attendance on religious study. Concededly,
> there are many parochial schools that do not impose
> such restrictions. Where they do not, it is even
> more difficult for me to understand why the primary
> effect of these statutes is to advance religion.
> (at 804)

Not accepting the appellants' stereotype of the parochial school, he would have allowed the aid program to continue.

11. *Sloan,* 413 U.S. 325 (1973).

In another decision invalidating a Pennsylvania plan to assist parents of parochial school children, a point was raised by Justice Powell that most of the children attending nonpublic schools in the State went to religiously affil- iated ones, "and most of these schools are affiliated with the Roman Catholic Church." (at 830)

Ball, arguing for the appellants, reminded the Court that:

> There is no record foundation for the figure 90%, nor has any witness, document, or admission been placed in the record to give substance and meaning to the words "controlled, religious organizations," "propagating and promoting," or "religious faith."[38]

His appeal for following standardized procedures of juris- prudence fell on deaf ears as the appellees' assertions were treated like factual findings by the majority of the Court.

12. *Wheeler,* 417 U.S. 402 (1974).

It is interesting to note that in this decision in which no negative profile of the parochial school was offered by the Court, the rights of parochial school children to "comparable" Title I services were affirmed by Justice Harry Blackmun in the majority opinion.

The respondents' brief argued that the LaNoue Paper and the "indicia of religiosity" proposed there could be classified only as "highly conjectural and speculative" and "based upon the most ephemeral sort of hearsay." The respondents also attacked LaNoue's personal background and predilections which could "scarcely qualify him as an impar- tial observer."[39]

These points of the respondents were well taken by
the majority. In a concurring opinion that has an air of
teasing about it, Justice White expressed his wonderment at
this apparent change in posture of the Court:

> . . . it is implied that there are programs and
> services comparable to on-the-premises instruction
> that the State could furnish private schools with-
> out violating the First Amendment. I would have
> thought that any such arrangement would be imper-
> missible under the Court's recent cases construing
> the Establishment Clause. Not having joined these
> opinions, I am pleasantly surprised by what appears
> to be a suggestion that federal funds may in some
> respects be used to finance elementary and second-
> ary schools. If this is the case, I suggest that
> the Court should say so expressly. (at 429)

13. *Meek,* 421 U.S. 349 (1975).

In yet another Pennsylvania case, the same positions
were brought forth as have appeared in other cases. Justice
Stewart delivered the opinion of the Court. It was held
that "the direct loan of instructional material and equipment has the unconstitutional primary effect of advancing
religion because of the predominantly religious character of
the schools benefiting from the Act." (at 363)

The oral argument and briefs of those opposed to the
Pennsylvania plan were taken over almost wholesale by the
majority of the Supreme Court, especially as the plan held
out the possibility of diversion of the secular aid to
religious ends, the need for surveillance of the secular
teachers, and the potential for conflict between publicly
paid teachers and the administrators of the religiously
oriented schools.

Berger's brief filed on behalf of the American Association of School Administrators expressed doubt that the
instructional equipment could not be "diverted to religious
purposes." Berger even suggested that laboratory equipment

"could be used in courses teaching a religious view of the
world about us."[40]   The oral argument followed the same line
of thought: "Maps, charts and globes, instructional materials specified in Act 195, can easily be used in connection
with a recruitment campaign for religious vocations and
missionary work."[41]   The witch-hunt tactics, remnants of
McCarthyism, were not repudiated by the majority of the
Court. On the contrary, they were endorsed: "The likelihood of inadvertently fostering of religion may be less in a
remedial arithmetic class than in a medieval history seminar
but a diminished probability of impermissible conduct is not
sufficient. . . ." (at 371)

Regarding the possibility that the religious administrators would dominate and unduly influence the publicly paid
teachers, Berger alleged that "it is not in reason to assume
that those responsible for the overall operation of a
school, and particularly for its functioning as an agency
for inculcation of a particular religion, will refrain
altogether from seeking to influence what goes on in classrooms."[42]   The oral argument of the appellants criticized
the "sustained administrative relationships necessitated by
the arrangement."   The appellants noted that the school
still "remains under the control and direction of the religious authorities and the public school teacher must work
out his or her operational relations with them on a continuing and day-to-day basis," resulting in a "master and
servant" relationship.[43]

The majority opinion picked up on all the issues cited
by the opponents of the plan and agreed completely:

> The fact that the teachers and counselors
> providing auxiliary services are employees of the
> public intermediate unit rather than of the church-
> related schools in which they work, does not
> substantially eliminate the need for continuing
> surveillance. To be sure, auxiliary services

personnel, because not employed by the nonpublic
schools, are not directly subject to the discipline
of a religious authority, but they are performing
important educational services in schools in which
education is an integral part of the dominant sectarian mission and in which an atmosphere dedicated
to the advancement of religious belief is con-
stantly maintained. (at 371)

Catholic school teachers came under fire in the AASA
brief, which indicated that the situation "would require
close and constant supervision."[44]   The oral argument likewise suggested the need "to continually review the content
of the teacher's instruction."[45]   The majority opinion of the
Court agreed and, in the most blatant affront to parochial
school teachers to date, went further to observe:

> For decisions of this court make clear that
> the District Court erred in relying entirely on
> the good faith and professionalism of the secular
> teachers and counselors functioning in church-
> related schools to ensure that a strictly non-
> ideological posture is maintained. (at 369)

In a dissenting opinion most sensitive to the problems
of parochial school students and parents, Chief Justice
Burger noted the following:

> There is absolutely no support in this record
> or for that matter, in ordinary human experience
> for the concern some see with respect to the
> 'dangers' lurking in extending common, nonsectarian
> tools of the education process--especially remedial
> tools to students in private schools. (at 385)
> The melancholy consequence of what the Court
> does today is to force the parent to choose between
> the 'free exercise' of a religious belief by opting
> for a sectarian education for his child or to
> forego the opportunity for his child to learn to
> cope with--or overcome--serious congenital learning
> handicaps, through remedial assistance financed by
> his taxes. . . . One can only hope that, at some
> future date, the Court will come to a more enlight-
> ened and tolerant view of the First Amendment's
> guarantee of free exercise of religion, thus elimi-

nating the denial of equal protection to children
in church-sponsored schools, and take a more
realistic view that carefully limited aid to children is not a step toward establishing a state
religion--at least while this Court sits. (at 387)

Justice William Rehnquist similarly called for the Court
to restrict itself to the record and also indicated his concern over the Court's negativity toward parochial schools:

    I find this portion of the Court's opinion
deficient as a matter of process and insupportable
as a matter of law. The burden of proof ordinarily
rests upon the plaintiff, but the Court's conclusion that the dangers presented by a state-
subsidized guidance counselor are the same as those
presented by a state-subsidized chemistry teacher
is apparently no more than an ex cathedra pro-
nouncement on the part of the Court, if one may
use that term in a case such as this, since the
District Court found the facts to be exactly the
opposite--after consideration of stipulations of
the fact and an evidentiary hearing. . . . (at
391f)
    I am as much disturbed by the overtones of the
Court's opinion as by its actual holding. The
Court apparently believes that the Establishment
Clause of the First Amendment not only mandates
religious neutrality on the part of government but
also requires that this Court go further and throw
its weight on the side of those who believe that
our society as a whole should be a purely secular
one. (at 395)

14. *Roemer,* 426 U.S. 736 (1976).

A Maryland aid program for colleges, including denominational ones, was held valid by this case in which Justice
Blackmun wrote the majority opinion. The profile of the
schools in question figured prominently again. The following characteristics formed that profile: (1) The colleges
were formally affiliated with the Roman Catholic Church,
but were "characterized by a high degree of autonomy;" (2)
Roman Catholic chaplains were hired for conducting services,
but attendance was not required, although spiritual develop-

ment of the students was encouraged; (3) Mandatory theology
classes were taught, but "in an atmosphere of intellectual
freedom;" (4) Some classes were begun with prayer; (5) "The
District Court found that, apart from the theology depart-
ments, faculty hiring decisions are not made on a religious
basis;" (6) The great majority of students are Roman
Catholics but students were "chosen without regard to
religion." (at 755-7)

Based on the image conveyed above, one would be hard-
pressed to demonstrate a much more "sectarian" picture in
one of the elementary or secondary schools. This awareness
prompted Pfeffer to criticize this distinction[46] and to
offer it as an illustration of his assertion that "the law
of Church-State relations abounds with legal fictions."[47]

Although Justice Stevens opposed the program in question, he offered a piece of advice that religious schools
would probably do well to ponder: "I would add emphasis to
the pernicious tendency of a state subsidy to tempt religious schools to compromise their religious mission without
wholly abandoning it." (at 775)

15. *Wolman*, 433 U.S. 229 (1977).

The Court held valid an Ohio statute aiding parochial
school pupils, with a few exceptions. Justice Blackmun drew
up a profile of the schools:

> It was also stipulated that, if they were
> called, officials of representative Catholic
> schools would testify that such schools operate
> under the general supervision of the Bishop of
> their Diocese; that most principals are members of
> a religious order within the Catholic Church; that
> a little less than one-third of the teachers are
> members of such religious orders; that 'in all
> probability a majority of the teachers are members
> of the Catholic faith;' and that many of the rooms
> and hallways in these schools are decorated with a
> Christian symbol. All such schools teach the secu-

lar subjects required to meet the State's minimum
standards. The State-mandated five-hour day is
expanded to include one half-hour of religious
instruction. Pupils who are not members of the
Catholic faith are not required to attend religion
classes or to participate in religious exercises or
activities, and no teacher is required to teach
religious doctrine as a part of the secular courses
taught in the schools.
     The parties also stipulated that nonpublic
school officials, if called, would testify that
none of the schools covered by the statute discriminate in the admission of pupils or in the hiring
of teachers on the basis of race, creed, color, or
national origin. (at 234-5)

The profile put forth by Blackmun was not the one
suggested by the appellants. Rather, it was that of the
appellees, who urged the Court to use the record and not a
hypothetical profile: "These stipulations demonstrate that
the Catholic schools in Ohio do not fit the standard profile
described in prior decisions of this Court and that the
heretofore presumed differences between elementary, secondary and higher education may need reconsideration."[48]

     Since the testing provided did not admit of teacher-made
tests, the Court held that provision of the law valid. (at
240-1) However, instructional equipment and field trips did
not fare as well:

     In view of the impossibility of separating the
     secular education function from the sectarian, the
     state aid [of equipment] inevitably flows in part
     in support of the religious role of the schools.
     (at 250)
     First, the nonpublic school controls the timing
     of the trips and, within a certain range, their
     frequency and destinations. Thus, the schools,
     rather than the children, truly are the recipients
     of the service and, as this Court has recognized
     this fact alone may be sufficient to invalidate the
     program as impermissible direct aid. Second,
     although a trip may be to a location that would be
     of interest to those in public schools, it is the
     individual teacher who makes a trip meaningful.

The experience begins with the study and discussion
of the place to be visited; it continues on
location with the teacher pointing out items of
interest and stimulating the imagination; and it
ends with a discussion of the experience. The
field trips are an integral part of the educational
experience, and where the teacher works within and
for a sectarian institution, an unacceptable risk
of fostering of religion is an inevitable by-
product. (at 253-4)

The concern over entanglement between parochial and
public school authorities regarding transportation emerged
directly from the brief of the appellants, who argued that
the trips depend "upon the unilateral determination of the
nonpublic school administrator as to the number and destina-
tion of field trips."[49] The loan of instructional equipment
was termed a "transparent fiction" by the Committee for
Public Education and Religious Liberty; the Court agreed.[50]

Justice Powell felt compelled to admit that "our decisions in this troubling area draw lines that often must seem
arbitrary." Nagel would certainly agree with Powell: "The
justices' confusion encourages further litigation, if only
in the desperate attempt to find out what they might mean.
. . . On any given Monday, if you catch the brethren in the
right frame of mind, you might win."[51]

Powell went on to discuss the role and purpose of
parochial education:

Parochial schools, quite apart from their
sectarian purpose, have provided an educational
alternative for millions of young Americans; they
often afford wholesome competition with our public
schools; and in some States they relieve substantially the tax burden incident to the operation of
public schools. The State has, moreover, a legitimate interest in facilitating education of the
highest quality for all children within its bound-
aries, whatever school their parents have chosen
for them. (at 262)

The fact that the parochial school is "at heart . . . religious" was sufficient for Justice Stevens to consider the entire Ohio program invalid. (at 265) Justice Thurgood Marshall, on the other hand, was concerned with the potential for divisiveness (raised in *Lemon*). He argued that "this danger exists whether the appropriations are made to fund textbooks, other instructional supplies, or, as in *Lemon*, teachers' salaries." (at 258) He further indicated his opposition to the testing program for the following reason:

> The counselors will also collect and organize the information for use by parents, teachers, and students. This description makes clear that paragraph (H) authorizes services that would directly support the educational programs of sectarian schools. It is, therefore, in violation of the First Amendment. (at 261)

In a footnote on the same page, he warned of the need to be "sensitive to the danger of subtle abuses" on the part of the counselors. It is strange that Marshall could not accept the logic of the appellants that the interaction of speech and hearing staff would result in possible indoctrination of the children,[52] especially since he was so concerned about "subtle abuses". Perhaps, though, the ridicule of this point of the appellants by the District Court had some influence: "To say that health services . . . must be held in silence in order to meet all constitutional objections strikes this Court as beyond the reach of reason."[53]

The connection between strict separationist attitudes regarding aid to parochial students and the respective justices' attitudes toward parochial schools was essentially maintained and reinforced in this case.

16. *Regan*, 444 U.S. 646 (1980).

Pfeffer once again led the opposition to efforts to upgrade education in all schools, public and private, through New York's Mandated Services Act. In the oral arguments, for which this researcher was present, Pfeffer reminded the Court that he had been fighting "parochiaid", as he termed it, since the very first case in 1947. The majority of the Court took a dim view of the reminder and even reacted skeptically, if not scornfully.

In his brief for the appellants, Pfeffer made much of the fact that the aid in question was given "directly to the schools;"[54] that even though the services paid for are state-mandated, this "is constitutionally irrelevant;"[55] that since no auditing of the parochial school books was envisioned by the legislation, the schools would "have a free hand to use the State funds to advance religion;"[56] that the administration of the examinations "may be used by overzealous teachers as a means to inculcate religious values,"[57] especially with the topic of evolution in Earth Science.[58] He brought the whole discussion to rest on his now-familiar fear that such legislation would result in "political entanglement and divisiveness along religious lines."[59]

Lewin and Rapps, on behalf of Yeshiva Rambam, reminded the Court of the "sectarian school's lack of control over the content of New York's standardized tests."[60] Abrams's brief pointed to the 200-year history of New York's having chartered nonpublic schools under the Board of Regents;[61] that "it is the competency of the writing *qua* English composition which is tested, not the content;"[62] that five percent of all tests are routinely returned to the State for review of correcting procedures.[63] Nolan's brief concluded that the entanglement envisioned by Pfeffer was merely limited to "the simple verification requirement imposed on any vendor to the State."[64]

Appellees argued their case rather well since the majority of the Court, with Justice White speaking for them, found the legislation constitutional. The majority opinion noted the legislative finding of New York State and quoted extensively from the District Court. The entire discussion essentially revolved around who controlled the preparation and grading of the tests; five justices saw the process controlled by the state and believed the process could not be diverted to religious ends. The majority likewise absolutely refused to accept the appellants' contentions regarding political divisiveness and even more that religion is so pervasive in a parochial school that any aid to such a school is *ipso facto* aid to religion.

Justices Blackmun, Brennan and Marshall, however, regarded the legislation as unconstitutional because they accepted Pfeffer's analysis of the situation, and most especially the notion that a parochial school's environment is totally permeated by religion. Justice Stevens would have dismissed the entire issue to discourage any further attempt at providing governmental assistance to nonpublic school children. In reacting to such attitudes, Regan (not the appellee) reflected on how sad it was "to note that so many justices still have so much difficulty identifying a secular objective in students learning to count, whether they learn to count angels or apples."[65]

It is also interesting to observe a word used repeatedly by the dissenting justices to describe what the majority of the Court in this case generally referred to as "church-sponsored" schools. The dissenters almost invariably classified them as "sectarian" institutions—no less than 22 times in barely nine pages of opinions. Over a decade ago

Lynn warned that this word "played a mischievous role" in Supreme Court decisions.[66]

It may never be fully known how much Pfeffer's reputation for hostility toward parochial schools finally convinced the majority of the inaneness and complete fancifulness of so many of his allegations. At the same time, one must acknowledge that his logic was accepted by four justices. Again, had one more justice been convinced by Pfeffer of the nature of parochial schools, the legislation would not have passed muster. Surely the identity of the schools was the telling issue.

Summary

While puzzling at best, the line of reasoning used to date suggests that no truly substantial programs of financial assistance for education in church-related schools will be seen as constitutional as long as Justices Brennan, Marshall, Blackmun, Powell and Stevens (or justices with attitudes like theirs) sit together on the Court. Since Justice Stewart usually voted with this block, how his replacement will vote is a matter of considerable interest and concern. Chief Justice Burger and Justices White and Rehnquist are definitely open to the constitutionality of governmental aid to the parents of children in nonpublic schools.

In every case cited, it can be readily seen how a justice's impression of Catholic schools leads to a final decision. Equally enlightening is the court's frequent reliance on sources with a history of anti-Catholicism or with a vested interest in opposing any program that would provide alternatives to government-run schools.[67] The emotionally charged language used (e.g., "creeping sectarianism", "zealots", "propagandists", "religious control",

"divisiveness", indoctrination", "idiosyncrasies", "prose-
lytizers"), the resultant tone of so many of the opinions,
the adamancy of the justices espousing negative attitudes
toward the Church and its schools, and the refusal to
accept information documented in the record all lead one to
question the goodwill and objectivity of justices who so
consistently decide cases not on constitutional grounds as
much as on vague or emotional impressions. The critical
question, however, is whether or not that impression is
based on reality.

NOTES

CHAPTER VI

[1]"If stereotypes and images of bigotry persist, the reason is that such symbols are very useful in interpreting and organizing experience when one does not have accurate information. Furthermore, if experience is sufficiently well organized by the symbols of bigotry, then one need not bother to gather information."
[Greeley, *Ugly Little Secret*, p. 40.]

[2]". . . the United States Supreme Court must examine the character and purposes of the institutions which are benefited, the nature of the aid that the state provides, and the resulting relationship between the government and the religious authority."
[*Lemon v. Kurtzman*, 403 U.S. 602 (1971).]

[3]Frank Sorauf, *The Wall of Separation* (Princeton: Princeton University Press, 1976), p. 215.

[4]*Ibid.*, p. 226.

[5]Richard Morgan, *The Supreme Court and Religion* (New York: The Free Press, 1972), p. 161.

[6]Robert Nagel, "A Plague of Judges," *The Human Life Review* 7 (Winter 1981): 110-111.

[7]Robert Bork, Hearings before the Subcommittee on Separation of Powers, Committee on Judiciary, U.S. Senate, June 1981, pp. 12-13.

[8]Jacob Cooke, ed., *The Federalist* (New York: World Publishing Co., 1961), p. 526.

[9]Saul Padover, *A Jefferson Profile* (New York: John Day Co., 1956), p. 154.

[10]*Ibid.*, p. 1173.

[11]William Douglas, *The Court Years* (New York: Random House, 1980), p. 81.

[12]"Insight Time," *National Review* 33 (1 May 1981): 471.

[13]*Zorach v. Clauson*, 343 U.S. 306 (1952).

[14]Justice Jackson, concurring in Illinois *ex rel. McCollum v. Board of Education,* 333 U.S. 238 (1948).

[15]Benjamin Cardozo, *The Nature of the Judicial Process* (New Haven: Yale University Press, 1921), p. 168.

[16]James Conant, *Education and Liberty* (Cambridge, Mass.:   Harvard University Press, 1953), p. 81.

[17]Whitney Seymour, Brief for the American Civil Liberties Union as amici curiae, *Everson v. Board of Education,* 330 U.S. 1 (1947).

[18]"A prime illustration of the divisiveness which inevitably results when the state intrudes into essentially private affairs occurred just last year when New Yorkers were asked to vote on a new constitution which contained, among many other provisions, a repeal of the constitutional ban on state aid to parochial schools."
[Marvin Pollack, Brief for the Appellants, p. 35.]

[19]*Ibid.,* p. 16.

[20]Henry Clausen, Brief for United Americans for Public Schools as amici curiae, *Lemon v. Kurtzman,* 403 U.S. 602 (1971), p. 11.

[21]Clausen, *How to Pauperize Your Public Schools,* Supreme Council, Mother Council . . . of Freemasonry, 1981.

[22]Leo Pfeffer, Brief for American Association of School Administrators, et al. as amici curiae, p. 11.

[23]Let two excerpts serve as examples of the anti-Catholicism typical of the work:
"It is a fact beyond challenge that the Protestant countries of Europe and the Americas have been comparatively strong, progressive, enlightened and free, while the Roman Catholic countries have remained relatively stationary or have stagnated and have had to be aided economically and politically by the Protestant nations.
"The lesson of history is that Romanism means the loss of religious liberty and the arrest of national progress." [p. 13]
". . . its [the Roman Catholic Church's] aggressive policy in infiltrating governments, schools, press, radio, etc., its lax moral code . . ." [p. 16]
[Loraine Boettner, Roman Catholicism (Philadelphia: Presbyterian and Reformed Publishing Co., 1974).]

[24]Franklin Fitzpatrick, "Supreme Court Vacancies and Catholic Schools," *The Tablet,* 30 September 1971, p. 1.

25"Here we see a Justice of the Supreme Court citing this as sociological, educational information.

"I suggest there is an insensitivity associated with such citations and that it portrays a mindset which has been insensitive for a very long time. It would be inconceivable to my mind that a comparable citation from the Ku Klux Klan or the Protocols of the Elders of Zion would pass unremarked in the public press.

"I would not mind had Justice Douglas cited a determined secularist saying that there should be no religious teaching in school, but the Justice cited the passage that said the Catholic schools teach the wrong religion. No doubt that is the view of many people, but it scarcely is the stuff of a Supreme Court decision."
[95th Congress, p. 13218.]

26Pfeffer, p. 3 *(supra,* note 22).

27Paul Blanshard, *American Freedom and Catholic Power* (Boston: Beacon Press, 1960), p. 80.

28George Kelly, ed., *Government Aid to Nonpublic Schools: Yes or No?* (New York: St. John's University Press, 1972), p. 91.

29Daniel Friedman, et al., Brief for the Appellees, *Tilton v. Richardson,* 403 U.S. 672 (1971), p. 24.

30*Ibid.,* p. 25.

31"I hope the Senators in opposition will address themselves to this proposition: The Attorney General has stated that tuition tax credit to a freshman in a Methodist college is constitutional; tuition tax credit to a senior in a Lutheran high school is unconstitutional. Now, I am sorry; if you believe that, you believe anything."
[95th Congress, p. 13205.]

32"This is from M. Brewster Smith, the president of the American Psychological Association, a long-established, much respected organization:

"There is no comparable comprehensive treatment of a religious change over the high school years that I know of, and while surely a close search might turn up scattered studies, I think it is fair to say, in answer to your question, that solid evidence regarding the high school vs. college comparison in which you are interested does not exist."
[95th Congress, p. 13200.]

[33]"It is not easy to justify the compromise on constitutional logic. . . ."
[Leo Pfeffer, *God, Caesar and the Constitution* (Boston: Beacon Press, 1967), p. 356.]

[34]William Ball, Brief for the Appellees, p. 26.

[35]Leo Pfeffer, Brief for the Appellees, *Levitt v. Committee for Public Education and Religious Liberty,* 413 U.S. 472 (1973), p. 25.

[36]Pfeffer, Brief for the Appellees, *Cathedral Academy v. Committee for Public Education and Religious Liberty,* 413 U.S. 472 (1973).

[37]Pfeffer, Brief for the Appellants, *Committee for Public Education and Religious Liberty v. Nyquist,* 413 U.S. 756 (1973), p. 24.

[38]William Ball, Brief for the Appellants, *Sloan v. Lemon,* 413 U.S. 825 (1973), p. 20.

[39]Thomas Sullivan, Brief for the Respondents, *Wheeler v. Barrera,* 417 U.S. 402 (1974), p. 79.

[40]Paul Berger, Brief for American Association of School Administrators, et al. as amici curiae, *Meek v. Pittenger,* 421 U.S. 349 (1975), p. 21.

[41]Leo Pfeffer and William Thorn, Oral argument in behalf of the Appellants, p. 27.

[42]Berger, p. 20 *(supra,* note 40).

[43]Pfeffer and Thorn, p. 20 *(supra,* note 41).

[44]Berger, p. 21 *(supra,* note 40).

[45]Pfeffer and Thorn, p. 19 *(supra,* note 41).

[46](f. *supra,* note 33).

[47]Pfeffer, *Church, State and Freedom* (Boston: Beacon Press, 1967), p. 194.

[48]David Young, Brief for the Appellees, *Wolman v. Walter,* 433 U.S. 229 (1977), p. 13.

[49]Joshua Kancelbaum, Brief for the Appellants, p. 52.

[50]Pfeffer, Brief for Committee for Public Education and Religious Liberty as amici curiae, p. 16.

[51]Nagel, p. 11 *(supra,* note 6).

[52]Kancelbaum, p. 25 *(supra,* note 49).

[53]U.S. District Court, Southern District of Ohio, Eastern Division, p. A21.

[54]Pfeffer, Brief for the Appellants, *Committee for Public Education and Religious Liberty v. Regan,* 444 U.S. 646 (1980), p. 10.

[55]*Ibid.,* p. 9.

[56]*Ibid.,* p. 11.

[57]*Ibid.,* p. 13.

[58]*Ibid.,* p. 20.

[59]*Ibid.,* p. 16.

[60]Nathan Lewin and Dennis Rapps, Brief for Appellee Yeshiva Rambam, p. 5.

[61]Robert Abrams, Brief for Appellees Regan and Ambach, p. 10.

[62]*Ibid.,* p. 34.

[63]*Ibid.*

[64]Richard Nolan, Brief for Appellee Schools, p. 33.

[65]Richard Regan, "Supreme Court Roundup: 1979 Term," *Thought* 55 (December 1980): 499.

[66]Robert Lynn, "The Eclipse of a Public," *Theology and Church in Times of Change* (Philadelphia: Westminster Press, 1970), p. 195.

[67]"To ensure that the penalty on religious exercise remains in force for Catholics, a new and powerful organization has now been formed. Called the National Coalition for Public Schools, it is comprised of 41 major national organizations claiming to represent more than 70 million people. . . .
"Many of its constituent organizations, such as the National Education Association and the American Federation of Teachers, have a vested interest in the demise of private schools. And others, such as

the American Civil Liberties Union and Americans United for Separation of Church and State, have a history of anti-Catholic prejudice. Opposition from these groups should come as no surprise."
    [Virgil C. Blum, "Enemies of Religious Freedom Join Forces," *Tablet,* 1 August 1981, p. 10.]

CHAPTER VII

HOW THE CHURCH VIEWS PAROCHIAL SCHOOLS

The work of this chapter involved the selection of certain key dioceses around the United States[1] to determine their policies and practices in regard to their parochial schools. Dioceses were chosen either because parochial school aid legislation from their states was challenged before the Supreme Court, or because of the researcher's desire to include a representative geographical overview of the country. Many dioceses have no policy handbooks for their schools, thus leaving each school to form its own policies. Several dioceses are in the process of updating their manuals to reflect new situations or new approaches. It is important to note that these handbooks not only state the ideal for Catholic education in a given diocese but actually have the force of diocesan law, having been approved and promulgated by the bishop.

In culling policy statements from the respective diocesan handbooks, the researcher kept in mind the elements of the profile which the Supreme Court had identified, trying to find material in the handbooks which would either substantiate or refute those elements. Several dominant elements emerge in what might be termed the Supreme Court's composite profile of the parochial school. Some of these should be noted here. According to the Court:

1. The schools are tied in to the structure of the diocese and are an extension of the magisterial authority of the bishop;

2. The superintendent of schools is a priest;

3. Religious instruction and worship are part of the normal school day;

4. An absolute, total permeation of the curriculum by religion is expected;

5. Secular instruction is offered, along with the religious;

6. Secular texts are normally selected to promote and advance Catholic doctrine, including specifically Catholic editions of various textbooks;

7. A majority of the faculties are clergy and religious, and certainly so at the administrative level;

8. A substantial portion of the school's activities are religiously oriented;

9. Formal religious instruction is presented for 30 minutes a day;

10. Identifying religious symbols are in evidence throughout the building;

11. The parochial school is located next to a parish church;

12. It is to be expected that parochial school teachers will evade state restrictions on the separation of religious and secular functions, either consciously or unconsciously;

13. Public employees working in a parochial school would experience the same difficulty as their parochial counterparts because of the over-riding influence of clerical or religious administrators who would, in all likelihood, pressure these individuals to disobey state regulations in this regard;

14. Parochial school teachers are religious "zealots".

This composite profile has valid and invalid elements within it. It would be foolish and dishonest for Catholic schools to deny that they are what they are supposed to be. Justice John Paul Stevens alluded to this in reference to the situation at the college level.[2] However, it is equally true that many of the items listed here are so exaggerated as to be sheer caricatures of both the stated goal and the reality. Still other descriptions are patently false and have their origins in the imaginations of the opponents of aid to parochial school parents.

Court Image v. Diocesan Image

Rather than repeat material unnecessarily, one should note that all the handbooks reviewed contained statements supporting the American bishops' pastoral letter on Catholic schools ("To Teach as Jesus Did"), and all emphasized the need to stress the three essential components of Catholic education: message, community, service. All likewise acknowledged that the bishop of the diocese was the general overseer of the schools as chief teacher in the diocese, with appropriate delegation of authority to a superintendent of schools and the respective pastors, where applicable.

1. In *Everson* the Court noted that the superintendent of schools was a priest. While that was undoubtedly the norm in 1947, such is no longer the case. In fact, no handbook reviewed even mentioned the canonical status of the superintendent. At present the chief educational officer for Newark is a nun, Trenton has a priest, New York's is a brother, and Washington has a layman.[3]

2. Religious instruction and worship are included within the activities of the normal school day. Most dioceses mandate 30 minutes of formal religion at the elemen-

tary level on a daily basis, with the day beginning and ending with prayer. However, variations exist even here. In the Diocese of Camden at the secondary level, the study of theology is required for all students:

> 607 Policy for the Requirement for the Study of Theology.
>
> "Since an educated person pursues an awareness of his or her environment and since any student, though not a Catholic, by attending a parochial school has chosen to be educated in the particular environment of the Catholic heritage, all students, Catholic and those of other faiths or no faith at all, will pursue the same or similar courses of academic study of Theology and will have the same academic requirements. (This is distinct from both proselytizing and preparation for reception into full communion.)"[4]

The Archdiocese of Minneapolis-St. Paul, on the other hand, lists as its religious education objectives:

> "to provide for the religious instructional needs of all our students regardless of religious beliefs;
> "to teach the basic truths of the Catholic faith to Catholic students." (PR-10)

Paterson strikes a position between Camden and Minneapolis-St. Paul:

> 5150.2 Non-Catholic Students.
>
> "If an applicant is not a Catholic, the school's religious program and its policy on non-Catholic students' participation should be explained to parents. Ordinarily, students should participate in religion classes, but may be excused from specific religious activities or programs at the request of parents."

Non-Catholic parents in Philadelphia archdiocesan schools actually sign a form "recognizing the obligation for the students to attend Religion classes and religious functions

offered as part of the school program during the week."
(305.5a)

A resolution of the Newark Archdiocesan School Board
states the following policy:

> "That the Catholic schools of the Archdiocese
> continue to pursue academic excellence in their
> program of studies, and include the further dimen-
> sion of a complete and organized curriculum in
> Religious Studies, that this program of Religious
> Studies be required of all Catholic students in
> each academic year, that the courses be graded and
> evaluated on a par with all academic subjects and
> necessary for graduation." (Policy #1)

Prayer and liturgical services likewise reflect the
full spectrum of possible policies. The archdiocese of
Cincinnati speaks in very general terms, thereby allowing
much latitude for local school decisions:

416.03 School Liturgical Celebrations.

> "Liturgy is integral to the Religious Program.
> The opportunity for each student to participate
> in Liturgy should be provided. Teachers and stu-
> dents have an important role in planning these
> celebrations."

416.04 Opening and Closing of the School Year-
         Eucharist.

> "At the beginning of each new school year, the
> staff and students are encouraged to celebrate the
> Eucharist together as a sign of their unity in
> Christ. At the end of each school year it is
> recommended that a Eucharist be celebrated as an
> act of thanksgiving for blessings received during
> the year."

Newark reveals a similar attitude:

> "Provision should be made for liturgical cele-
> brations, especially the Eucharist, on a large and
> small group basis with student and faculty par-
> ticipation encouraged.
> "Other types of religious programs including
> days of recollection, communal celebration of
> penance, scripture services and para-liturgical

celebrations, designed to foster and exemplify the
faith should be scheduled by the Principal with the
cooperation of local priests. Parent participation
at such programs is highly recommended.
    "Daily compulsory Mass attendance during school
time is strongly discouraged." (0411)

In Philadelphia the same kind of regulation is in evidence:

515   Liturgical Experiences.

    ". . . it is expected that the parish and the
school will make participation in the liturgy and
the sacraments readily accessible to its students,
developing personal sanctity and building a community of faith."

However, the Archdiocese, at the secondary level, has an
additional regulation (#330) providing for the possibility
of expulsion for a student who, after repeated attempts by
school officials to seek correction, continues to neglect
Sunday Mass on a regular basis.

    The varied approaches to formal liturgical worship
carry over into the requirements on the place of prayer in
school.

Paterson:

7150   Prayer.

    "In general the school day should always begin
and end with prayer. So, too should class periods
and assemblies. . . ."

Portland:

6141.2   Recognition   of   Religious   Beliefs   and
         Customs.

    "Catholic schools must develop in their stu-
dents a commitment to community and to the social
skills and virtues needed to achieve it. Participation together in the liturgy and in para-
liturgical activities and spiritual exercises can
effectively foster community among students and
faculty.

"Teachers and students are encouraged to open
and close each school session with appropriate
prayers of their own choosing.
    "Any pressure, real or apparent, to require the
reception of the sacraments would be most inappro-
priate. Proper motivation in the performance of
religious duties should be stressed.
    "Students should be led into a variety of
prayer experiences in addition to the learning of
formal prayer."

Providence:

    134-G Prayer in School.

    "The nature of prayer and the implementation of
the action of prayer must be taught from time to
time in our religious studies classes.
    "Each school day should open with prayer--
formally--by the homeroom teacher, or spontaneously
by students, or quiet private prayer.
    "Each class should open with prayer. These
prayers may be formal, i.e., official prayers of
the church or composed by the department of religious studies, or they may be done spontaneously by
students or done privately and quietly by all in
the classroom.
    "All faculty and departmental meetings should
be opened with a prayer.
    "All school assemblies should be opened by
prayer.
    "Each moderator and/or coach should invite
their students to pray before undertaking their
respective activities."

Different philosophies among the dioceses is clear even from
the verbs used: "should", "must", "encouraged", "invite".

    3. A major concern of the Supreme Court has been that
the entire curriculum of a Catholic school is permeated by
the Catholic philosophy of life. The word "permeation" is
rarely used by the dioceses in question. Some never discuss
the issue; others speak of an "integrated curriculum."[5] Let
the following serve as examples:

Camden:

603 Curriculum Policy.

"A goal of the program of instruction in the
schools of the diocese is to provide learning
experiences which integrate religious truths and
values with the intellectual, social and physical
development of the student."

Newark:

0701 Instructional Objectives.

"The primary goal of the program of instruction
is to provide learning experiences in a Catholic
environment which will assist the students in their
religious, moral, intellectual, social, emotional
and physical development."

Chicago:

4123.1 Organic Curriculum.

"The content and the process of learning should
be consistent with the way modern man experiences
reality. For this reason, the school should as a
matter of practice explore the interrelatedness of
all subject disciplines forming alliances across
subject field lines whenever and wherever possible.
It should develop instructional plans, materials,
and the whole physical environment of the school in
such a way that the belief in the integration of
all learning is manifest in the program that
children experience. Schools should reflect the
belief that children learn in different ways and at
different times. Most especially, the religious
dimension of Catholic Education should be witnessed
to in every aspect of the instructional program.
'Sacred' and 'secular' are not two separate areas
of reality, but two different ways of looking at
the same reality."

New York:

621 Primary Goal.

"The primary goal of the program of instruction
in the schools of the Archdiocese is to provide
those learning experiences which most effectively
inculcate worthwhile attitudes and impart the
knowledge and skills necessary for the spiritual,

intellectual, emotional, and physical development
of the student."

Cincinnati:

Sixth Synod (Archdiocese of Cincinnati, 1971).

"The whole atmosphere at the school is to be a
Catholic one, animated by a community of faith--the
children, the teachers and the parents." (p. 97)
"What the Catholic school does, ideally, is to
offer the opportunity for a searching exploration
of religious values and beliefs, ideally, too, it
does so in a structured setting--a school commu-
nity--where these values are lived out as well."
(p. 99)

Philadephia:

400   Instruction and Curriculum.

[In this entire section religion is never
mentioned, except for the time allotment for religion in the daily schedule for 30 minutes a day in
primary and increasing to 45 minutes in the upper
grades. (435)]

Providence:

001   Rationale for Catholic Schools.

"The Roman Catholic Diocese of Providence
operates its schools from its conviction that religious beliefs and values are an integral part of
the educational process and that without these
religious beliefs and values, education is very
strongly defective. Religious beliefs and values
serve two purposes within the school. First, they
are a subject. Second, they are the integrating
factors in the school environment which enable a
child to make sense of what he learns in school and
of his total life experience."

Trenton:

Philosophy Statements:

". . . Therefore, the Christian/Catholic principles taught in the home will be reinforced and
expanded by the school.
"It is within the Catholic school that children
can experience learning and living fully integrated

in the light of faith. Catholic schools afford the
fullest and best opportunity to realize the three-
fold purpose of Christian education--message,
community, service--among children and young
people.
"The integration of religious truth and values
within the curriculum is brought about by the
presence of administrators and teachers who express
this integrated approach in their private and professional lives.
"Therefore, the mission of the Catholic schools
in the Diocese of Trenton is dedication to the
development of programs which more fully convey
the message of Christ and create a climate where
academic excellence is pursued."

The point of home-school cooperation hit upon by the
Trenton Diocese is critical because the Supreme Court seems
to have the impression that parochial schools impose a
philosophy or worldview which is, somehow or other, alien or
novel to the child's experience. The contrary is the case:
the Church's schools present a certain worldview because
they have been deputed to do so by the child's parents. The
Archdiocese of Newark put it thus:

0802 Parental Involvement.

"The home is the first school where a child
learns of love and respect for God and man. Parents
in choosing a Catholic school to continue the education begun at home, have responsibilities as well
as opportunities to share in the continuance of
thier children's education.
"At the level of school policy, parents may
serve on a parish Board of Education. In a less
formal, but nonetheless important level, is the
local Home-School Association involvement. Each
level offers parents an opportunity to be actively
involved in their child's educational situation."

The second area of concern to the Court has been that
the permeation is absolute and affects the educational process in such a way that the secular educational objectives of
the State may not be realized. Two areas of concern need to
be addressed in that regard.

First, assuming that the religious permeation of the curriculum is total (which experience demonstrates is not the case, for how else to explain later defections from the Church by Catholic school graduates?), would that substantially alter the achievement of basic academic skills or qualities of citizenship? It is obvious that the academic goal is not subverted because Catholic school students take competency tests with their public school counterparts and fare as well, if not better (cf. New York's Regents exams). Blum saw the situation in this way:

> A religious permeation of secular subjects no more changes their secular character than a dye changes the cotton fabric of a woman's blouse. . . . If there were in fact a Protestant grammar, a Catholic geography, a Jewish chemistry, and a Secularist algebra, how would high school seniors of church-related schools qualify for the National Merit Scholarship competition in which all students take the same tests?[6]

In other words, it should matter little whether a child learns to count the beads on an abacus or on a rosary, so long as the child learns to count. That loyalty to American ideals and the democratic way of life is instilled in Catholic school children needs no support beyond a quick look at the historical record of Catholic school alumni who have served in the military with distinction and in numbers greater than other religious groups, and by the ever-increasing number of Catholics serving their nation in Congress, now the largest denomination represented.

The second problem area, however, is that the Supreme Court has difficulties with a religious environment for education because it seems to believe that value neutrality is possible in the educational enterprise. Once again experience proves otherwise.[7] Not to speak of a topic or a person is to deny it subtly but effectively. The approach to education envisioned and countenanced by the Court, and practiced by the nation's public schools over the past decade and a half comes closest to secular humanism,[8] which the Court has identified as a philosophy of life entitled to protection under the First Amendment's religion clauses.[9] What the Court is doing, then, is to favor one philosophy of life over another and thereby to penalize those who do not opt for the one in favor--a situation which should never develop if the First Amendment is properly interpreted.[10]

Since educators and psychologists alike know that value-free education is impossible, and one assumes the Court has been apprised of this, the only conclusion possible regarding the permeation question and the Court is not that the justices object to values being taught in school but that they object to certain values being taught. Inasmuch as they have chosen to address themselves only to Catholic parochial schools, one may also assume that the certain values to which they so strenuously object are Catholic values.

4.   The Court has noted on numerous occasions that parochial schools offer secular instruction as well as religious education. Needless to say, all the school policy manuals devote a majority of their pages to the secular educational process. Listed as the first goal of a Catholic school for the Archdiocese of Chicago is: "to enable students to acquire basic skills, especially in the art of communications, in quantitative thinking and the sciences." (#4112.1)

The Archdiocese of Dubuque notes:

6003 B2. Academic Area.

"The Academic subjects of the elementary and secondary schools are as required by Minimum Educational Standards for Approved schools of Iowa." (Code of Iowa 257.25)

5. No diocesan policy handbook has any reference whatsoever to selecting Catholic textbooks for secular subjects, in spite of the insistence of certain members of the Court that this is done and, in fact, inevitable. Dioceses in which state texts are available follow state regulations here as elsewhere. The Diocese of Providence is a good example of this kind of policy:

16-23-2 Loan of Textbooks.

117-G (State Regulation)

The school committee of every community as the same is defined in (Sec. 16-7-16) shall furnish upon request at the expense of such community, textbooks in the field of mathematics, science and modern foreign languages appearing on the published list of textbooks recommended by the commissioner of education as provided in 16-1-9 of the general laws, as herein amended, to all pupils of elementary and secondary school grades resident in such community, said textbooks to be loaned to such pupils free of charge, subject to such rules and regulations as to care and custody as the school committee may prescribe."

117a-G Length of Use of Textbooks.

"Textbooks should not be changed at the suggestion of new faculty members unless the expiration date of the currently used books coincide with the arrival of new faculty members. Principals should set specific periods of time for use of particular books; e.g., Social Studies texts might be used in a school for three years. In the case of State Aid textbooks, our schools should follow the local public school policy on the length of use of these texts."

6. That a substantial portion of the school's activities are religiously oriented finds no basis in the directives set down by the respective dioceses. In fact, most handbooks rather carefully limit what kinds of religious involvement are permitted, so as not to detract from the overall educational program:

Camden:

1002 Co-Curricular Activities.

"The assignments for serving or singing at
funerals during school hours should be rotated so
that no student is taken out of the classroom more
frequently than is necessary. The practice of
relying on the same group of boys and girls for
every funeral is unfair to them, to their teachers
and to their parents.

"Instruction and practice for altar boys and
choir is to be held outside of school hours."

[Encouragement for other kinds of co-curricular
activities like mission work, Catholic Youth
Organization, field trips "to places of historical
or educational significance" and athletic events is
provided for in 1003, 1004, 1005, 1006.]

Providence:

411-E Altar Boys.

"Where it is deemed necessary to call on the
services of elementary grade students to serve at
the altar of the parish church, the local principal
will make every effort to cooperate with the
pastor. Principals and pastor, or his representative, should plan the altar boy schedule to make
certain that the same students are not called too
frequently from classes to serve at liturgies.
Students who fall behind in their school studies
should be assigned to weekend liturgies. As a rule
liturgical rehearsals should be held outside of
school time."

7. The Court is quite correct in its statement that
formal religion classes are offered. These classes are at
least 30 minutes' duration. A general rule seems to be
the one enunciated by the Paterson Diocese: "The time
allotted to formal classroom teaching of religion should be
comparable to that time given to other major subjects."
(#7120)

8. The presence of religious art work and aids to
devotion has also been mentioned by the Court. This is, in
all likelihood, a fair representation of the facts although

only two handbooks specifically allude to this matter. The Diocese of Trenton calls for the crucifix to be displayed in every classroom, along with the American and papal flags. (#6114) The Camden Diocese discusses the question in terms of room decoration and treats it in the context of providing an integrated learning environment, so that the religious element is simply included among other types of possible display materials:

613 Display Boards.

"Bulletin boards, tack boards, ply boards, strips of corkboard over chalkboards can be very effective teaching aids in the classroom. For optimum use, materials should be changed every few weeks and related to the subject matter. Feature posters, specimens of pupils' work, art work celebrating the liturgical seasons, and displays depicting current issues such as Respect Life and Social Justice are suitable subjects for display and can be of great value in creating a learning environment in the classroom and school."

9. There is no evidence in the handbooks for the Court's assertion that parochial schools are located next to parish churches. The statement is, in the majority of cases, accurate since parishes usually build a total plant on one tract of land, but there is no necessity for having a Catholic school situated near a church. Diocesan and private high schools would not be so situated because they are generally constructed as independent entities with no canonical or financial relationship to any given parish.

10. Surely one of the most damaging allegations made by the Supreme Court is that parochial school teachers will evade, consciously or unconsciously, state restrictions on the separation of religious and secular functions. The Court has never supported this opinion with fact; however, facts to the contrary can be brought forward by a reading of the diocesan handbooks. All the manuals discuss state regu-

lations with respect; civic duties and citizenship training are likewise treated. A brief survey under three headings would be instructive: respect for the flag and what it represents; desire for obedience to federal regulations; concern for forming students who will appreciate and contribute to their states and local communities as citizens fully committed to democratic principles.

°*The Flag*

The display of the flag is referred to in nearly every manual. The rationale offered is usually similar to the one offered by the Archdiocese of Dubuque:

6115.1 Ceremonies and Observances.

Flag of the United States

"The Flag of the United States of America should be displayed during school days in and near every school.
"Display of the flag fulfills Public Law 829 and Code of Iowa, Section 280.4.
"The Code of Iowa reads:
"The board of directors of each public school corporation and the authorities in charge of each private school shall provide and maintain a suitable flagstaff on every school site under its control, and a suitable United States flag, therefore, shall be raised on all school days when weather conditions are suitable. [(Iowa Code (1954), 280.4)]
"It is recommended also that a flag of the United States be displayed in every classroom.
"Teachers should seek opportunities to guide students to an understanding of the symbolism of the flag, an appreciation of the concepts and values portrayed, and an attitude and manner of respect for the flag."

°*Federal Regulations*

The dioceses are most diligent in counseling obedience to federal law relating to eduation. Many handbooks even quote these regulations verbatim, especially those dealing

with equal opportunity and integration. A sampling of
quotations from the various handbooks should demonstrate the
point.

Philadelphia:

> 305.1 High School Admissions Policy.
>
> ". . . No student is to be admitted if there
> is any indication that the parents and student are
> seeking admission to flee a racial situation in the
> public or private school."

Newark:

> 0422 Student Records In Federal Programs.
>
> "If a Catholic School directly receives a grant
> in its own name through the Education Division of
> the U.S. Office of Health, Education and Welfare,
> then the school is required to comply with the
> student record procedures of Public Law 93-380,
> Section 513, called the 'Family Educational Rights
> and Privacy Act of 1974.'"
>
> 0603 Admissions.
>
> "There shall be no discrimination with regard
> to race, color, national origin or ethnic back-
> ground in determining eligibility for admission."

Trenton:

> 5111 Admissions.
>
> In accepting students in any Catholic school
> within the Diocese of Trenton, state and federal
> regulations that apply must be followed. (Titles
> VI and IX)"

Portland:

> 4111 The Archdiocese As An Equal Opportunities
> Employer.
>
> "In hiring new teachers, principals, pastors
> and school boards are advised that the Archdiocese
> of Portland is an Equal Opportunites Employer."

5111   Equal Opportunities.

"The Catholic schools of the Archdiocese of Portland admit students of any race, color, national and ethnic origin to all the rights, privileges, programs, and activities at all schools. They do not discriminate on the basis of race, color, national or ethnic origin in administration of its educational policies, admissions policies, scholarship and loan programs, and athletic and other school administered programs."

Paterson:

4110.10   Minority Groups.

"Administrators should make positive efforts to recruit teachers from minority groups."

5230.4   Students of Minority Groups.

"Students of minority groups, regardless of religious affiliation, shall be admitted to the elementary and secondary schools of the diocese without the usual requirements of residency, or national heritage, or parish membership. The only requirement shall be average ability and available space. A positive effort should be made by every school to develop specific programs to meet the needs of these students."

8200   Title IX, Sex Discrimination.

". . . . This law affects all institutions which receive aid even indirectly and, as such, applies to Catholic schools."

Minneapolis-St. Paul:

AR-3   Discrimination.

"It is the policy of the Catholic Schools of the Archdiocese of St. Paul and Minneapolis to comply with federal and state laws prohibiting discrimination and all requirements imposed by or pursuant to regulations issued thereto, to the end that no persons in any school listed below . . . shall on the grounds of race, color, national and ethnic origin, sex(*), marital status, status with regard to public assistance, age, or disability be excluded from participation in, be denied the benefits of, or be otherwise subjected to discrimination under any educational program, or in employment, or recruitment, consideration, or selection, whether parttime or fulltime, under any educational program, employment, or activity operated by the school."

"(*)Single-sex schools are exempt from the above requirement as they apply to selection of incoming students."

Dubuque:

4005 B. Equal Opportunity.

"The Educational System of the Archdiocese of Dubuque is committed to equal opportunity and does not discriminate on the basis of race, color, national and ethnic origin, or sex in the educational programs, or activities which it operates. The Educational System policy not to discriminate in educational programs and activities, extends to employment in and admission to such programs and activities and services. It admits both employees and students of any race, color, national and ethnic origin or sex to all rights, privileges, employment opportunities, programs, activities, and services generally accorded or made available in the programs/activities. It does not discriminate in the administration of its educational policies, employment policies, admission policies, scholarship and loan programs, athletic, and other school administered programs."

Cincinnati:

501.00 Admissions Policy.

"No student may be excluded from a Catholic school solely because of race, color, religion, national origin, or ancestry.

"Catholic schools have a positive obligation from the Gospel message to promote and encourage racial integration in order to help provide for the total educational experiences of students in the school.

"As required by Title IX of the Educational Amendments of 1972, a school shall not discriminate on the basis of sex in its admission policies or educational program."

Chicago:

3111   Integration.

"The Archdiocese of Chicago School Board is firmly committed to high quality integrated education. Integration remains a priority objective of the school in order to prepare children to live, work and develop in a nation and world which are multi-racial. Furthermore, since the parochial schools of the Archdiocese are an integral part of the larger society of metropolitan Chicago, and since de facto segregation weakens the fabric of society, the parochial schools will make their proper contribution toward eliminating a dual system of schools based on racial difference."

Providence:

402-G   Student-Diocesan Position on Education of.

"The Diocese of Providence supports the ideal of a Christian education for every Catholic Christian child who desires it. No student shall be denied admission to any school in the Diocese on the basis of race."

Washington:

2510   Nondiscrimination.

"Schools in the Archdiocese of Washington, mindful of their primary mission as effective instruments of the educational ministry of the Church, and the witnesses to the love of Christ for all--shall not discriminate on the basis of race, color, national or ethnic origin in the administration of educational policies, personnel policies, admissions policies, loan programs, and athletic and other school-administered programs."

2520   Sex Nondiscrimination.

"Schools in the Archdiocese of Washington, mindful of their primary mission as effective instruments of the educational ministry of the Church, and the witnesses to the love of Christ for all--will not discriminate against any applicant/ employee because of sex; and will not discriminate against any student because of sex in any educational program and activity.

"This policy does not preclude having schools which enroll only boys or only girls."

4112 Appointment of Personnel.

Personnel shall be employed without discrimination as to race, sex, or national origin. All qualifications being equal, Catholic teachers will receive priority for appointment."

As can be readily seen, the respective dioceses have not simply advocated adherence to the letter of the law, but have given added impetus by spelling out a clear diocesan commitment and rationale for the principles enshrined within the laws.

°*State and Community Obligations*

As the policy handbooks discuss federal regulations, so too do they deal with state education laws. The handbooks are also concerned that teachers educate their charges in such a way that, as adults, they will be ready to assume roles of leadership and responsibility in a democratic, pluralistic society.

Cincinnati:

003.00 State Standards.

"Any educational program offered in a Catholic school should meet or surpass the minimum standards specified for such a program by the State Board of Education."

105.02 Qualifications: Principals.

"Should meet requirements for an Ohio state Principal's certificate as indicated in the Minimum Standards."

227.00 Professional Growth.

The State Department of Education obligates every elementary and secondary school to provide for the professional growth of its staff members."

511.01 Reporting Attendance to Public School Officials.

"Any pupil who is repeatedly absent from school without an acceptable excuse should be referred to the Attendance Department of the local public school for investigation by a Visiting Teacher."

New York:

411 Qualifications.

"Current New York State certification requirements for teachers are followed in the schools of the Archdiocese of New York. The State Education Department requirements for certification including the 1978 amendments are in the appendix (A411)."

421 Oath of Allegiance.

"According to the Education Law (Section 3002) of New York State, every teacher is required to take an oath pledging his/her support of the Federal and State Constitutions. On beginning service in an Archdiocesan school, each teacher is required to take an Oath of Allegiance and to complete the form indicating that this has been done (A421)."

500 Attendance.

"The education law of the State of New York requires that each person from six to seventeen years of age attend school on a full-time basis. At age sixteen a student may be discharged from school, if he/she has a full-time employment certificate.

"Legally there is no minimum number of days that an individual student must attend school.

"Strict legal requirements exist regarding the number of days a school must be in session. New York State requires that each school be in session at least 180 days, inclusive of three days spent by teachers at professional conferences approved by the superintendent of schools."

Register of Attendance.

"Each school is required by New York State law to keep for each pupil on register an accurate record of daily attendance, absence, and lateness.

In the Catholic elementary school the register of attendance is used for record keeping. This attendance register must be kept in the school building; it should not be taken home by teachers. The register of attendance must remain on file for fifty years."

Newark:

Archbishop's Cover Letter.

"The guidelines provided herein are not intended to restrict the operation of our schools, but rather to facilitate the proper management of these schools in keeping with goals of Catholic education and the New Jersey statutes.

0402 Commemoration of Historic Events.

"The spirit of patriotism should be developed by the remembrance and celebration of significant persons and events in the historical beginnings and growth of our country. Films, assemblies, plays, civic programs and other legitimate means of celebration are encouraged on such days."

0404 Fire Drills.

According to New Jersey School Law it shall also be the duty of every Principal and janitor of a school building having a furnace room, hallways or stair-tower fire or smoke doors, to keep them closed during the time the building is occupied by teachers and pupils."

0405 Health and Safety Regulations.

"Health, sanitation, fire and law enforcement officials should be received with courtesy and cooperation and their recommendations should be complied with as completely as possible."

0423 Discipline.

"Corporal punishment is forbidden under New Jersey Statute and must be avoided diligently."

0604 Absence.

"The New Jersey Statutes on Education (18A. 38-5) provides for compulsory attendance by all children between the ages of six and sixteen, but the responsibility for compliance belongs to the parents. The school is required to keep accurate records of daily attendance, tardiness and absence. All entries in the Attendance Record shall be made only by the teacher or by a school clerk designated by the Principal. This Record must be kept in the school building at all times.

"When the child has been absent, the school must require a written excuse from his parents. These notes must be kept on file for one year. If a pupil is absent without an excuse, or if the school has reason to suspect the validity of an excuse, the situation should be investigated. Cases of frequent absenteeism should be referred to the attendance officer of the local public school district."

0701 Goals.

"11. To develop a sense of responsibility for the community in which they live.
"12. To develop an appreciation for the heritage, responsibilities and privileges of the American Society.
"13. To become aware of the interdependence of all the nations of the world."

0702 Programs.

"1. New Jersey State Law.
New Jersey State Law requires the following courses of study be included in the elementary curriculum:
"Instruction in accident and fire prevention (18A:6-2)
"Constitution of the United States (Gr. 7 and up) (18A:6-3)
"Civics, Geography and History of New Jersey (18A:35-3)
"Alcohol and Narcotics, nature and effects (18A:35-4)
"Principles of Humanity (18A:35-4.1)
"Health, Safety and Physical Education (18A:35-5, 35-7)
"Career Development Programs (18A:35-4.2)"

0801 Statement of Purpose.

"Catholic schools do not operate in isolation. Rather, they are dependent on a broad spectrum of groups within and outside the Archdiocese and the parish for support, assistance and services.

State, county and local governments, municipal
groups, school authorities--public and Catholic--
parish societies and associations, the parish and
the community at large all have an interest and
concern with the operation of the schools.

"Relationships with all of these groups are
necessary, in greater or lesser form, if the school
is to operate effectively. Administrators, faculty, students and parents are required, therefore,
to foster such contacts and communications as are
necessary to maintain a mutually beneficial relationship with all groups concerned."

0901 Relations with Public School Authorities.

"The Catholic School is part of the community
in which it is situated and has a stake in that
community's welfare. Since both the Catholic
Schools and the Public Schools seek to provide
education for the community, the lines of communication are required to be open between the
Principal and the local public school Superintendent. A working relationship and, where applicable, coordination with the public school is
encouraged. Periodic participation at public board
meetings by the Principal and/or parent representatives would increase awareness of the educational
issues in the school district particularly those
that may affect the Catholic Schools. Appropriate
responses may be developed or action initiated as a
result of these contacts."

Trenton:

1321 Public Performance by Students.

"The Diocesan Office of Education recognizes
that worthy and appropriate educational values
accrue from pupil participation in civic and community events."

6120 Goals of the Instructional Program.

"Courses should present an objective and
balanced picture of the ethnic and religious groups
making up our pluralistic society. Subjects taught
in the schools must be brought to the child in a
way that will permit him/her to grow mentally,
physically, socially, spiritually and emotionally."

Chicago:

4112 Goals.

"9. to assist each student in his efforts to make a place for himself in the neighborhood community and in the larger society."

"13. to provide for all students educational opportunities and experiences which emphasize the heritage, the responsibilities and the privileges of American citizenship."

Philadelphia:

Philosophy Statements.

"1. The parish elementary schools of the Archdiocese of Philadelphia serve the family, the Church, the parish and the State by helping students fulfill their religious and educational potentials."

600 Relationships between Parish Elementary Schools and Public Schools.

"Public and parish elementary schools have their own character and philosophy, which must be mutually respected. Since both types of institutions serve the same general community, and are an important force for good within that community, it is important that a wholesome spirit of cooperation should exist and should be evident to the community. As a matter of professional responsibility, each principal should be acquainted with his or her public school counterpart and should regularly consult with the public school officials on matters that affect either or both the schools. . . ."

Providence:

001 Goals.

"6. to generate in our students the spirit of ecumenism with members of other Christian groups as well as with non-Christian groups."

"7. to admit into our schools, interested and qualified underprivileged students of minority groups."

16-38-10   Power of Officials to Visit Schools.

009   (State Regulation)

"Any school receiving aid from the state, either by direct grant or by exemption from taxation, may be visited and examined by the school committee of the town in which such school is situated, and by the board of education or its duly authorized agents, whenever they shall deem it advisable."

111-G   The School Day.

"The definition of a school day is the same as that given by the State Board of Education."

116-G   Fire Drills.

"Catholic schools shall follow the State Regulations on fire drills."

118-G   State Testing Program.

"The schools of the Diocese will follow the State-Wide Testing Program. State tests must be administered at the grade levels indicated by the Commissioner of Education in his directive according to State Regulation 118. Complete information regarding this testing program will be issued from the Catholic School Office at the appropriate time."

Department of Health--Department of Education-- Rules and Regulations:

In Accordance with the provisions of Chapters 21, 22 and 38 of Title 16 of the General Laws of Rhode Island, 1956, as amended, rules and regulations are hereby adopted to implement and administer the school health program. [Seven pages of detailed regulations from the State that apply to parochial schools are included.]

It seems reasonable that any diocese which would go to the trouble of detailing civil laws and civic responsibilities would hardly encourage its teachers to disregard federal or state regulations in the next breath. Nor is there any record of such encouragement in manuals, memos or conference addresses. Absent any proof for the allegations of the Supreme Court, one must conclude that the Court believes it is so merely because they believe it is so.

11. The Court has also said that the ideological problems to which parochial school employees are subject would just as easily befall public employees working in a parochial school. The matter of such employees is discussed nowhere in any diocesan manual. However, if the assertions of the Court are groundless in reference to full-time parochial school teachers, how much more so would they be for publicly hired and salaried teachers working within clearly defined governmental programs for parochial school children?

12. Parochial school teachers are religious zealots, the Court has declared. The term "zealot" conjures up images of Jonestown and other cult-related situations. One needs to determine if the dioceses are looking for such individuals to teach in and administer their schools. The Supreme Court has also observed the presence of large numbers of clergy and religious on the faculties, especially in administrative positions. Once more the diocesan policy handbooks reveal some interesting facts.

Camden:

303 The Teacher.

"The Catholic school teacher is a person of faith, a community builder and a leader in Christian service who is carefully prepared both in secular and religious knowledge which can be conveyed to the students who are assigned to the teacher's classroom."

Chicago:

2112.3 Religious Standards.

"Because the distinctive and unique purpose of the Catholic school is to create a Christian educational community--one enlivened by a faith that is shared among teachers and students--it is expected that teachers employed in the Archdiocesan elementary schools will be Catholics who have a knowledge of and commitment to the Catholic faith and to Christian living.

"At the same time it is recognized that teachers of other faiths, who themselves are committed to the religious education of youth can make exemplary contributions to the spirit of the Christian educational community."

Dubuque:

4010 B.   Religious Education Requirements.

"It is essential that those teaching in Catholic schools have a background in scripture, theology and religious education. Graduates from a non-Catholic college are expected to take courses to build up necessary background. Likewise, all teachers need to continue education of a religious nature in order to keep themselves updated. All are to participate in spiritual renewal experiences available to them."

Paterson:

1110.4   Objectives Pertaining to Teachers.

"3. To provide in each school a faculty who, while treasuring the rich heritage of the Church, continue to explore the current research of educators, theologians, and psychologists, thus continually seeking greater enrichment and enlightenment."

4110.2   Teacher Standards.

"Given the fact that teachers in a Catholic school teach religious and moral values not just in religion class, but throughout the school day, it is resolved by the Diocesan School Board that practicing Roman Catholics be primarily hired as teachers in the schools of the Diocese of Paterson."

Portland:

4111.1   Religious Standards.

"The distinctive and unique purpose of a Catholic school is to create and foster a Christian community--one enlivened by a faith that is shared among teachers and students. Ordinarily, it is expected that teachers employed in the Archdiocese elementary schools will be Catholics who have a knowledge of and commitment to the Catholic faith and to Christian living.

At the same time it is recognized that teachers of other faiths who themselves are committed to the religious education of youth, can make exemplary contributions to the spirit of the Christian educational community."

538   Parish and Secondary School Relationships.

"It is desired that the principals and teachers be ever mindful of their students' parish life and make every effort to build within the students a deep sense of parish and Diocesan loyalty. Schools should invite the clergy of parishes served by the school to participate in the school's program in Religious education through dialogue with students. Schools should likewise invite parish clergy to assist at parents' nights, awards nights, honors programs and at other school activities that might be of interest to the clergy."

Providence:

101a-G   Principal--Employment of.

"The success or the failure of a school depends in great part upon the educational leader-- the principal. It is of the greatest importance that only qualified persons be chosen to lead in a school. A qualified applicant for the position in any of the schools of the diocese is one whose philosophy of education is in tune with the philosophy of the Catholic community and who, by experience elsewhere or as a teacher, has shown that he/she is knowledgeable of the latest trends in education-- both administrative and curricula wise."

302-G   Teacher--Values of.

"Any teacher engaged to teach in a school of the Diocese must be united in philosophy and objectives with Catholic values.

1. A Catholic teacher, divorced or remarried, should not be hired to teach, or allowed to continue to teach, in a Catholic school of the Diocese.

2. A Catholic lay teacher, married outside the Church, should not be hired to teach, or allowed to

continue to teach, in a Catholic school of the Diocese."

Trenton:

1710 Ecclesiastic Authority.

"Since a Catholic school, by its very definition, bears a special relationship to the pastoral
mission of the Church, school personnel should
strive to maintain clear and cordial relationships
with ecclesiastical authority."

Note: In the entire 2000 section, no requirement
is made for any employee at any level of teaching
or administration to be a Catholic.

4112.1 Contract.

"Contracts may be terminated during the
contract period by the Catholic school for the
following reasons:
"1. Failure to fulfill professional responsibilities as expressed in the school and diocesan
handbooks.
"2. Conduct unbecoming a teacher within the
Catholic schools of the Diocese.
"3. Failure to comply with the written philosophy and policies of the school."

Newark:

Board Policy, E1.

"Teachers of Religion must be persons of faith,
witnesses of the Gospel, and practicing Catholics
who desire to share their belief with their students. A prime requisite for all teachers of
Religion in our schools is that they are committed
believers in the teachings of the Roman Catholic
Church."

[Note: Teachers of Religion should be understood
as distinct from teachers of secular subjects.]

0303.20 Qualifications for Principals.

[Professional criteria are outlined, with no
necessity of being a Catholic--although the can-
didate is expected to understand and support the
Catholic philosophy of education.]

From the dioceses surveyed, it is clear that those hired as teachers and administrators in Catholic schools are expected to have a professional preparation equal to that of their public school counterparts, if not beyond it. These educators are also normally to be committed Catholics in good standing in the Church; at the same time nearly every diocese has a recognition of the contribution possible from non-Catholic teachers.

No manual calls for administrators to be chosen from the ranks of the clergy or religious. Furthermore, none even has an absolute requirement that administrators be Catholics. It would be safe to say, nonetheless, that the vast majority of teachers are Catholic laity, while the majority of the administrators are clergy or religious. However, administrative positions are being filled more and more by laity as the number of religious declines and the self-esteem of the laity increases to the point that lay leadership for Catholic schools is very acceptable in the Catholic community.

"Zealot" is an emotionally charged word. Whether or not one is a zealot is open to personal interpretation. The image of the parochial school educator suggested by the diocesan school policy manuals is not that of a zealot, in the opinion of this researcher.

A Study in Contrasts

The 14 elements that make up the Supreme Court's impression of Catholic education are of varying degrees of importance and validity. The Court is correct in identifying Catholic schools as institutions tied in to the structure of a diocese, under the authority of the local bishop. They are places where religious formation, worship and secular instruction take place in an integrated program;

they all fulfill state educational requirements. All these valid impressions likewise form the core of the reality of Catholic education, which cannot and should not be denied.

Other items in the composite image have little or no basis in reality. Clergy and religious form part of the teaching force, but by no means are they in the majority.[11] While the majority of parochial school personnel are Catholics, there is no absolute need for them to be Catholic.

No evidence exists to show that secular texts are chosen to support a particularly Catholic viewpoint in the secular subjects. That a substantial portion of the school's activities is religiously oriented raises the problem of defining "substantial". The location of the schools is not significant, nor is it necessary that they be in proximity to a church.

The most significant objections raised by the Court revolve around the issue of religious permeation of the curriculum and the lack of trustworthiness on the part of Catholic educators due to religious zealotry. The first issue can be dealt with in two ways: (1) by the schools' demonstrating that the permeation is not absolute; or (2) by challenging the Court to explain how even an absolute permeation would undermine the State's legitimate educational objectives.

To assert that any class of citizens is untrustworthy requires, under normal democratic principles, proof of the assertion. The Court has merely noted that since this possibility exists, a significant danger exists at the same moment--so significant that any aid tendered those institutions or parents using those institutions is an unconstitutional infringement of the First Amendment.

It is interesting to observe that what Catholic educators consider to be the critical elements of their educational process are provable and are not seen as, *ipso facto,* constitutionally problematic by the Court. However, what the Court considers critical elements are not provable and are, in their opinion, constitutionally problematic. An impasse of significant dimensions needs to be resolved.

NOTES

CHAPTER VII

[1]The (arch)dioceses included were: Camden, Chicago, Cincinnati, Dubuque, Minneapolis-St. Paul, Newark, New York, Paterson, Philadelphia, Portland-Oregon, Providence, Trenton, Washington.

[2]*Roemer v. Board of Public Works,* 426 U.S. 775 (1976).

[3]Respectively, Sr. Doris Ann Bowles, Msgr. Thomas Leubking, Br. James Kearney, Dr. Leonard DeFiore.

[4]The same holds true of the Diocese of Providence (#508).
[Note: The numbers listed either before or after a policy statement refer to that policy's number and location within the diocesan handbook.]

[5]"We would argue, however, that the defenders of a common core curriculum which excludes religion are doing injustice to the inter-relations between the forms of knowledge.   If the forms are logically interrelated, then it is impossible to divorce religion completely from the rest of the forms."
[Elmer J. Thiessen and L. J. Roy Wilson, "Curriculum in the Church-State Controversy," *Inform* 3 (January 1981):   4.]

[6]Daniel D. McGarry and Leo Ward, eds., *Educational Freedom and the Case for Government Aid to Students in Independent Schools* (Milwaukee: Bruce Publishing Co., 1966), p. 153.

[7]"That values are taught implicitly in schools is irrefutable.   Both the visible and the invisible (or 'hidden') curriculum of the school testify to this.   The lessons taught via the hidden curruculum, in fact, are so pervasive that many scholars have argued that they have far more influence than the lessons taught via the formal curriculum can ever hope to have."
[Jack R. Fraenkel, "Why a Comprehensive Program of Values Education Is Needed," *Social Education* 45 (19 February 1981):   101.]

[8]See: T. P. Draney, "The Humanist Manifesto," *The First Amendment and the Freedom of Religion in Education* (Albany: Catholic School Administrators Association of New York State, 1975), p. 28.
Note also: "Humanism: The attitude of mind which attaches primary importance to man and to his faculties, affairs, temporal aspirations and well-being. . . .

"In the 20th Century some new senses were given to the word humanism. F. C. F. Schiller (1864-1937) took it as the special name for his own version of pragmatism, maintaining that all philosophical understanding stems from human activities. . . ."
[*Encyclopedia Brittanica* 1975 ed., s.v. "Humanism."]
The public school "represents a body of intellectual, moral, and philosophical values based on the concepts that created it and [is] expressed in the activities that go on within its walls. The youngster who passes through its classrooms emerges indoctrinated in a body of secular values as if he had gone to a sort of governmental parochial school."
[Samuel Blumenfeld, *Is Public Education Necessary?* (Old Greenwich, Ct.: Devin-Adair, 1981), p. 3.]

9"Among the religions in this country which do not teach what would commonly be considered a belief in the existence of God are Buddhism, Taoism, Ethical Culture, Secular Humanism, and others."
[*Torcaso v. Watkins,* 367 U.S. 488 (1961), footnote at 495.]

10See: Chapter IV, Section 2, of the present work.

11Statistics from the National Catholic Educational Association for 1980-1981 reveal that 74.2% of the teachers were lay persons at the elementary level and 70.5% at the secondary level.
[NCEA Data-bank]

CHAPTER VIII

CONCLUSIONS AND RECOMMENDATIONS

Findings of the Study

The principal findings of the study may be grouped around the respective chapter headings.

Research into the public policy question revealed that:

1. Ample precedents exist for governmental financial aid to nonpublic school parents.

2. Serious misinformation is frequently passed on relative to nonpublic schools. It is important to realize that other than government schools can educate citizens in a democracy; that private schools generally, and Catholic schools in particular, are not segregationist academies; that parochial schools do not teach only religion.

3. Aid to nonpublic school parents would help improve the quality of education in all schools, by heightening competition between the public and private sectors, with the result being a boon to the total educational process in both sectors.

4. Programs of financial assistance would, both long-range and short-range, bring about savings to taxpayers at all levels--local, state, and federal.

5. Many opponents of aid to nonpublic school parents have developed their stance, not for constitutional reasons but for reasons of anti-Catholic animosity since the prime

beneficiaries of any such aid would be Catholic parents and, by extension, the Catholic Church.

6. One of the problems in recent years has been a tendency of the judicial branch of government to overrule the legislative branch. The present issue has been a victim of this conflict.

7. Governmental control of nonpublic schools need not go hand in hand with financial assistance; however, such a development is a real possibility.

8. A changing social consensus indicates increasingly favorable attitudes among the American people for programs that would provide financial aid for nonpublic school parents.

9. Pluralism has risen dramatically as an American value. Furthermore, pluralism in society-at-large requires pluralism in education to reflect the many publics that make up the total American population.

10. If parents are the primary educators of their children, they must have the ability to decide on the most appropriate educational environment for their children. As a matter of sound public policy, the exercise of that fundamental right should not be contingent on the ability to pay for the exercise of the right.

The constitutional aspects of the problem can be considered from the Constitution itself, from history, and from the opinions of the Supreme Court of the United States. The study brought to light the following facts:

1. The Supreme Court has allowed various types of aid programs to pass contitutional muster, under the child-benefit theory, and has even under certain circumstances permitted direct aid to the nonpublic schools.

2. The Court has developed a tri-partite test to determine the constitutionality of an aid program: a secular purpose; a primary effect that neither advances nor inhibits religion; no potential for excessive entanglement, administrative or political, between Church and State.

3. The First Amendment's prohibition of an establishment of religion was primarily designed to keep an established and governmentally sponsored national church from coming into existence.

4. The "no establishment" clause was meant to serve the "free exercise" clause for the flourishing of freedom of conscience.

5. The testimony of other western democracies stands as proof that separation of Church and State is possible even if denominational schools receive governmental support.

6. The first century and a quarter of this nation's existence found only denominational schools, all of which received tax support. Further evidence of this is the fact that so many states followed New York's example of enacting "Blaine Amendments" to forbid such aid in the 1860's and beyond.

Difficulties with financial aid for nonpublic school parents have surfaced at the Supreme Court level, where the Court has made two serious mistakes in stereotyping Catholic education as a monolithic system. The first is the Court's belief that parochial school teachers cannot be trusted to obey state-imposed regulations on the teaching of secular subjects for which aid might be given. The second mistake centers on the Court's over-whelming interest in the question of religious permeation of the total curriculum. The data shows either that absolute permeation is not a goal or that, even if it is, it does not hinder the achievement of the State's secular educational objectives.

Yet another insight gained from the study was the strong and consistent relationship that exists between a justice's image of the parochial school and how he votes on a given case before him. In every case cited, justices who spoke of parochial schools in positive terms voted for continuance of the respective aid programs. Conversely, those unfavorably disposed toward these schools voted accordingly. Also important to note is that most of the negative elements in the parochial school profile have come from special interest groups or groups with a history of anti-Catholic bias.

The review of diocesan school policy handbooks demonstrated a wide range of policies, with a great deal of latitude allowed to schools even within a diocese. Citations were brought forth from the manuals to substantiate and refute assertions of the Supreme Court. The strongest and most negative statements of the Court, however, found no diocesan support.

Such were the principal findings of this study. How they should find expression in the formation of law and public policy is the ultimate test of their worth.

Recommendations

Pure research is interesting, but the American pragmatic mind always seeks to put research to use. This is certainly true in the present situation. The facts and findings of the study are fascinating in and of themselves; more fascinating, however, is the vision of where these facts could lead this nation in the future. Based on the findings, the researcher presents recommendations for several potential audiences.

°*The Supreme Court of the United States*

If nonpublic school parents are to receive financial assistance from governmental sources, significant changes will have to occur within the members and the chambers of the Supreme Court. This researcher respectfully urges the following for the consideration of the Court:

1. To sense and act upon a changing social consensus among the American people on this issue;

2. To return to a more historical and less biased interpretation of the "no establishment" clause of the First Amendment, for, as the Court itself has said, "The comment that 'a page of history is worth a volume of logic' has special relevance"[1] here. This approach would bring about an enhancement of the "free exercise" clause, which should be dominant;

3. To restrict their opinions to the record rather than to allow themselves to be unduly influenced by conjecture;[2]

4. To receive briefs from anti-Catholic groups with the same kind of careful scrutiny that they would exercise in entertaining assertions of fact about blacks from the Ku Klux Klan or about Jews from the American Nazi Party;

5. To exercise what Kilpatrick has referred to as "judicial restraint,"[3] deferring to the other branches of government in such a way that makes clear that the American system consists of three coequal branches and not a judicial despotism;[4]

6. To view religion more broadly so that those for whom religion involves more than the home and the sanctuary will be able to practice their faith without penalty, thus eliminating what Shaw has termed "selective separation,"

whereby the Court promulgates "principles which, whether by accident or design, work selectively against the interests of some religious groups but not all;"[5]

7. To discover the connection between real freedom and economic freedom, so that the Court will uphold state and federal assistance for the exercise of basic constitutional rights;[6]

8. To see the need for a pluralistic society to have a plurality of educational forms, so long as those forms are consonant with basic democratic principles;[7]

9. To recognize the impossibility of maintaining a monolithic image of "the parochial school" by understanding the tremendous diversity which characterizes Catholic education from diocese to diocese, and even from parish to parish within a given diocese;

10. To look to the success of programs like Title I and Title IV of the Elementary and Secondary Education Act when attempting to discover parochial school personnel's attitudes and behavior patterns, rather than to accept hypothetical guesswork;

11. To rediscover the kind of government neutrality the First Amendment mandates vis a vis religion,[8] rather than the continuance of the kind of hostility which so concerned Justice Rehnquist in *Meek;*[9]

12. To identify and isolate their own personal biases as they impact on nonpublic education and the Catholic Church.

°*Nonpublic School Personnel and Parents*

If the ultimate decisions on this matter rest with the Court, the critical foundations must be laid by those who know and appreciate nonpublic education best: its administrators, teachers, parents and supporters. Since the vast majority of nonpublic schools are still Catholic, these recommendations are specifically geared toward the Catholic community although many of them are applicable to the non-public sector in general. Some necessary tasks are:

1. To do an effective public relations job by providing good and accurate information on private schools to the general public as the best way to combat negative stereotypes;

2. To respond to inaccuracies in the media with confidence, courtesy and firmness;

3. To develop and fund an organized lobby to represent the interests of nonpublic school parents, and to counterbalance the efforts of groups like the American Federation of Teachers and the National Education Association;

4. Never to deny the Catholic identity of Catholic schools for the sake of aid;

5. Never to accept arbitrary or unreasonable governmental regulations as conditions for aid, so that the private sector would simply become a carbon copy of the public sector;

6. To seek aid for parents, and not schools, in order to obviate the problems raised above (in 4 and 5), to stress the importance of parental freedom of choice in education, and to eliminate the need for extensive and often fruitless discussions on separation of Church and State;

7. To anticipate and deal with in advance the possible problems of decreased parental involvement and/or teacher commitment should financial aid be forthcoming;

8. To form ecumenical coalitions to diffuse the "Catholic issue" aspect of the question, thus having learned a lesson from history;[10]

9. To work with special diligence to have federal legislation enacted, rather than state laws, since it eliminates the necessity of 50 state battles and further, because the Supreme Court seems to be more hesitant to invalidate Congressional legislation.

°*Legislative Bodies*

Since any aid programs will develop through the legislative process, some practical suggestions would be helpful for legislators at both the state and federal levels:

1. To include legislative findings and intent, so that challenged legislation can be viewed by judicial reviewers in the correct light;[11]

2. To draft carefully worded bills which take into consideration constitutional and unconstitutional elements of similar legislation and to avoid pitfalls, always providing for severability which would salvage constitutional aspects of a bill if other aspects could not pass constitutional muster;

3. To be responsive to their constituencies, and to realize that Catholics and other nonpublic school advocates are organizing and expect their concerns to move up higher on the priority list of their legislators;

4. To assume their rightful role as a coequal branch of government, refusing to defer to the courts before they have even spoken on an issue;

5. To seek out and follow the example of other free nations in regard to parental freedom of choice in education;

6. To view the legitimate state interest in education as education *per se* and not necessarily as public education;

7. To sponsor programs like Tuition Tax Credits and/or the voucher plan, in order to maximize parental freedom of choice.

°*Public School Personnel*

Any discussion of federal financial assistance to non-public school parents would be incomplete without reference to public schools and their personnel. Recommendations to them include the following counsel:

1. To be open to programs that maximize parental freedom of choice in education without reflecting paranoiac fears of a mass exodus from public education, and without subtly expressing a desire to maintain a constituency for their schools by holding parents and students hostage through financial pressure;

2. To improve levels of discipline and learning, so that an exodus will not occur should a program like Tuition Tax Credits be enacted;

3. To accept private educators as partners in the American educational enterprise,[12] and to divest themselves of monopolistic characteristics;

4. To refuse to use scare tactics (like the exodus myth) to thwart aid programs for nonpublic school parents;

5. To be more secure in their own achievements and in their own special role in the overall educational process.[13]

Future Directions

This study sought to answer the question of what the constitutional possibilities are for governmental financial assistance to nonpublic school parents. Some limited aid has already been enacted into law and has been declared constitutional (e.g., transportation, textbook loans, diagnostic services, standardized tests). The criteria set by the Court are not completely clear; however, it seems that "conceivably any aid to the secular functions of sectarian schools will not be prohibited if the Court is assured it will be used for secular purposes and no on site surveillance is required."[14]

As this study is being completed, Congress is debating the future of Tuition Tax Credits. It is also known that Heritage Foundation's recommendations to the Reagan Administration include a voucher experiment.[15]

The most important aspect of the entire issue is not whether or not a specific piece of legislation is passed; nor is it important that large sums of money be involved. What does matter is that the broad topic of parental freedom of choice in education be raised on a consistent basis, so that the general population becomes sensitized to this fundamental human and civil right, guaranteed by the natural law and the Constitution of the United States. The basic realization that must become current in the thinking of the American people is that "when the rights of some are denied, the rights of all are imperiled."[16] The Supreme Court once saw this very clearly: "Freedom of speech, freedom of the press, freedom of religion are available to all, not merely to those who can pay their own way."[17]

If the Court sees parental choice of a parochial school as an exercise of religious freedom rights, which should never be infringed except in the face of a clear and present danger, the constitutional possibilities for governmental financial assistance to nonpublic school parents are virtually boundless.

NOTES

CHAPTER VIII

[1]*Committee for Public Education and Religious Liberty v. Nyquist,* 413 U.S. (1973).

[2]"In *Allen* the Court refused to make assumptions, on a meager record, about the religious content of the textbooks that the State would be asked to provide."
[*Lemon v. Kurtzman,* 403 U.S. 617 (1971).]

[3]James J. Kilpatrick, "Conservativism at the High Court," *National Review* 33 (7 August 1981): 895.

[4]"Congress currently has before it more than 30 bills designed to sharply restrict the authority of the Federal judiciary and limit its power to interpret the Constitution."
[Irving R. Kaufman, "Congress v. the Court," *New York Times Magazine,* 20 September 1981, p. 44.]

[5]Russell Shaw, "Arguments, Attitudes and 'Aid'," *Momentum* 6 (December 1975): 37.

[6]Surely this was the rationale behind the Supreme Court's declaring the poll tax in the South to be unconstitutional. See: *Harper v. Virginia State Board of Elections,* 383 U.S. 663 (1966).

[7]". . . unless it could somehow be shown that private schools will not reflect parents' wishes or that parents will wish to train their children in un-American ways, there may be grounds for wondering, but no grounds for acting as though private schools are a threat to desirable democratic unity."
[Robert L. Cunningham, *Education: Free and Public* (Wichita: Center for Independent Education, 1962), pp. 15-16.]

[8]"By extending aid to all institutions that serve the secular purpose of the government's program, whether public or private, church-related or not, the government is being neutral. . . . Indeed, it would be less neutral and would be discriminatory on religious grounds if it withheld assistance from church-related institutions only."
[Paul G. Kauper, *Religion and the Constitution* (Ann Arbor: Louisiana State University Press, 1964), p. 108]

[9]*Meek v. Pittenger,* 421 U.S. 395 (1975).

[10]". . . Catholics, under the leadership of some bishops made the fatal mistake of fighting the school question as a Roman Catholic question rather than as a question of a desirable exercise of parental rights."
[Cunningham, p. 19 (supra, note 7).]

[11]The importance of this has been stressed frequently:
a) ". . . the statute's statement that it is intended to enhance the quality of secular education in all schools covered by compulsory attendance laws must be accorded appropriate deference, where there is nothing undermining the stated legislative intent."
[Lemon v. Kurtzman, 403 U.S. 602 (1971).]
b) "The establishment of religion clause of the First Amendment does not foreclose a practical response by the state to the logistical difficulties of extending needed and desired aid to all the children of the community, including children attending sectarian schools."
[Wolman v. Walter, 433 U.S. 232 (1977).]
c) "There is a good chance it [the Court] will decide the matter on the basis of congressional intent."
[Russell Shaw, "A New Church-State Clash in the Offing?" Columbia 61 (April 1981): 33.]
d) "It is clear that the Court often defers to stated legislative intent in the secular purpose test."
[Judith Taylor, "Educational Vouchers: Addressing the Establishment Clause," Pacific Law Journal 11 (July 1980): 1072]

[12]". . . growing segments of the population now view private schools as the 'new public schools,' in the sense that these private schools are compatible with family and community values. . . ."
[Donald Erickson, The New "Public" Schools (Wichita: Center for Independent Education, 1977), p. 3]

[13]"They do some things that public schools can't and others that public schools shouldn't."
[Dennis A. Williams, et al., "The Bright Flight," Newsweek 97 (20 April 1981): 73.]

[14]Terry C. Cupps, "Schools: Permissibility of Direct Governmental Aid to Sectarian Schools," Washburn Law Journal 20 (Fall 1930): 185.

[15]Richard Brookhiser, "What Do Conservatives Want?" National Review 33 (6 February 1981): 82.

[16]Eugene Krasicky, "Ride in the Back of the Bus," Catholic Mind 74 (April 1976): 43.

[17]Cantwell v. Connecticut, 310 U.S. 111 (1940).

REFERENCES

Abbot, Walter M. and Gallagher, Joseph, eds. *The Documents of Vatican II*. New York: Guild Press, 1966.

Abington v. Schempp, 374 U.S. 203 (1963).

Abraham, Henry J. *Freedom and the Court*. New York: Oxford University Press, 1976.

Abram, Morris B. "Competitive Education: Giving Parents and Children Freedom of Choice," *Washington Post*, 11 September 1976, p. A15.

Abrams, Robert. Brief for Appellees Regan and Ambach, *Committee for Public Education and Religious Liberty v. Regan*, 444 U.S. 646 (1980).

Adamo, Salvatore, "Can Catholics, Jews Unite?" *National Catholic Reporter*, 27 January 1978, p. 11.

American Enterprise Institute for Public Policy Research. *Tuition Tax Credits and Alternatives*. Washington: American Enterprise Institute, 1978.

Antieau, Chester, et al. *Freedom from Federal Establishment*. Milwaukee: Bruce Publishing Co., 1964.

Arons, Stephen. *The Separation of School and State: "Pierce" Reconsidered*. Wichita: Center for Independent Education, 1977.

Ball, William B. Brief for the Appellants in *Sloan v. Lemon*, 413 U.S. 825 (1973).

_____. Brief for the Appellees, *Lemon v. Kurtzman* (Lemon II), 411 U.S. 192 (1973).

_____. "Constitutional Implications and Considerations: 'Board of Education v. Allen'," *Proceedings . . . National Meeting of Diocesan Attorneys*. Washington: United States Catholic Conference, April 1969, pp. 12-18.

_____. "Family Freedom in Education," *The Human Life Review* 6 (Summer 1980): 60-69.

_____. *Litigation in Education: In Defense of Freedom*. Wichita: Center for Independent Education, 1977.

Ball, William B. "Religious Liberty in Education," *Journal of Ecumenical Studies* 14 (Fall 1977): 662-676.

Barnes, William R., ed. *The Constitution of the United States and the Declaration of Independence* (annotated). New York: Barnes and Noble, 1965.

Baron, Alan. "Special Report: The Battle over Tuition Tax Credits," *The Baron Report,* 28 April 1981.

Bayley, Joseph. "Private Schools, Public Tax," *Eternity* 29 (May 1978): 71-72.

Beggs, David W., and McQuigg, R. Bruce. *America's Schools and Churches: Partners in Conflict.* Bloomington, Ind.: Indiana University Press, 1965.

Benabarre-Vigo, Benigno. *Igual Subvencion Estatal a las Escuelas Publicas y Privadas.* Madrid: Stadium, 1969.

Benestad, J. Brian. "The Political Vision of Pope John Paul II: Justice through Faith and Culture," *Communio* 8 (Spring 1981): 3-19.

Bennett, John C. *Christians and the State.* New York: Chas. Scribner's Sons, 1958.

Berger, Paul, et al. Brief for the American Association of School Administrators, et al. as amici curiae, *Meek v. Pittenger,* 421 U.S. 349 (1975).

Berns, Walter. *The First Amendment and the Future of American Democracy.* New York: Basic Books, 1976.

Billington, Ray Allen. *The Protestant Crusade.* New York: Macmillan, 1938.

Black, Charles L. *Structure and Relationship in Constitutional Law.* Baton Rouge: Louisiana State University Press, 1969.

Blanshard, Paul. *American Freedom and Catholic Power.* Boston: Beacon Press, 1960.

_____. *Religion and the Schools.* Boston: Beacon Press, 1963.

Blum, Virgil C. *Catholic Education: Survival or Demise?* Chicago: Argus Publications, 1969.

Blum, Virgil C. *Education: Freedom and Competition.* Chicago: Argus Communications, 1967.

_____. "Enemies of Religious Freedom Join Forces," *The Tablet,* 1 August 1981, pp. 10-11.

_____, ed., *Freedom in Education.* Garden City, New York: Doubleday and Co., 1965.

_____. *Freedom of Choice in Education.* Glen Rock, N.J.: Paulist Press, 1963.

_____. "Tax Refunds for Tuition," *America* 144 (11 April 1981): 294-297.

Blumenfeld, Samuel L. *Is Public Education Necessary?* Old Greenwich, Ct.: Devin-Adair Co., 1981.

_____. "Why the Schools Went Public," *Reason* 10 (March 1979): 18-23.

Board of Education v. Allen, 392 U.S. 236 (1968).

Boettner, Loraine. *Roman Catholicism.* Philadelphia: The Presbyterian and Reformed Publishing Co., 1974.

Bork, Robert. Hearings before the Subcommittee on Separation of Powers, Committee on Judiciary, U.S. Senate, 1 June 1981.

Bradfield v. Roberts, 197 U.S. 291 (1899).

Brady, Joseph H. *Confusion Twice Confounded.* South Orange, N.J.: Seton Hall University Press, 1955.

Brant, Irving. *James Madison: Framer of the Constitution.* New York: Bobs-Merrill Co., 1950.

Braunfeld v. Brown, 366 U.S. 599 (1961).

Breaching the Wall of Separation between Church and State. Church of Scientology of California, 1980.

Brickman, William W. *Subsidized Pluralism in American Education.* New York: Society for the Advancement of Education, 1959.

_____, and Lehrer, Stanley, eds. *Religion, Government and Education.* New York: Society for the Advancement of Education, 1961.

Brookhiser, Richard. "What Do Conservatives Want?" *National Review* 33
    (6 February 1981): 82.

Buckley, William F. "Black Leaders Off-Course on Education," *Inform* 2
    (November 1980): 4-5.

Buetow, Harold. *Of Singular Benefit*. New York: Macmillan Co., 1970.

Burns, James A., et al. *A History of Catholic Education in the United
    States*. New York: Benziger Brothers, 1937.

Burrup, Percy E. *Financing Education in a Climate of Change*. Boston:
    Allyn and Bacon, 1977.

Butts, R. Freeman. *The American Tradition in Religion and Education*.
    Boston: Beacon Press, 1950.

_____. "Education Vouchers: The Private Pursuit of the Public Purse,"
    Phi Delta Kappan 61 (September 1979): 7-9.

_____. "Public Funds for Parochial Schools? No!" *Teacher's College
    Record,* October 1960, pp. 57-62.

_____. *The Revival of Civic Learning*. Bloomington, Ind.: Phi Delta
    Kappa Educational Foundation, 1980.

Byrnes, Lawrence. *Religion and Public Education*. New York: Harper and
    Row, 1975.

Caldwell, Cleon. "The Development of Concepts Regarding the Use of Tax
    Funds for Public and Parochial Schools." Ph.D. dissertation,
    University of Minnesota, 1956.

Camden, Diocese of. *Elementary and Secondary School Policy Manuals,*
    1979.

Cantwell v. Connecticut, 310 U.S. 296 (1940).

Cardozo, Benjamin N. *The Nature of the Judicial Process*. New Haven:
    Yale University Press, 1921.

*Cathedral Academy v. Committee for Public Education and Religious Lib-
    erty,* 412 U.S. 472 (1973).

Chandler, Porter. Brief for Appellant Nonpublic Schools, *Cathedral
    Academy v. Committee for Public Education and Religious Liberty,*
    413 U.S. 472 (1973).

Chicago, Archdiocese of. *School Policies and Administrative Guidelines for Elementary Schools,* July 1979.

Choper, Jesse H. "The Establishment Clause and Aid to Parochial Schools," *California Law Review* 56 (1968): 260-341.

Cincinnati, Archdiocese of. *Archdiocesan Handbook of Policies,* 1979.

Clausen, Henry C. Brief for United Americans for Public Schools as amici curiae, *Lemon v. Kurtzman,* 403 U.S. 602 (1971).

_____. *How to Pauperize Your Public Schools.* Supreme Council, Mother Council of the World Ancient and Accepted Scottish Rite of Free-masonry, 1981.

Clymer, Adam, "Carter Budget Gets Support in Survey," *New York Times,* 31 January 1979, p. 1+.

Cogdell, Gaston D. *What Price Parochiaid?* Silver Spring, Md.: Americans United for Separation of Church and State, 1970.

Cogley, John, ed. *Religion in America.* New York: Meridian Books, 1958.

Coleman, James, et al. *Summary of Major Findings for Public and Private Schools.* Washington: National Center for Education Statistics, 1981.

"The Coleman Report," *America* 144 (25 April 1981): 335-336.

Committee for Public Education and Religious Liberty v. Nyquist, 413 U.S. 756 (1973).

Committee for Public Education and Religious Liberty v. Regan, 444 U.S. 646 (1980).

Committee on Human Rights of the National Citizens Commission on International Corporations. *For All Humanity.* New York: American Jewish Committee and United Nations Association, 1966.

Committee on Ways and Means (House of Representatives). *Tax Treatment of Tuition Expenses.* Washington: U.S. Government Printing Office, 1978.

Conant, James B. *Education and Liberty.* Cambridge, Mass.: Harvard University Press, 1953.

Confrey, Burton. *Secularism in American Education*. Washington: Cath-
    olic University of America Press, 1931.

Connell, Christopher. "School Study Rates Private over Public," *Courier-
    Post,* 4 April 1981, p. 2A.

Connelly, James F., ed. *The History of the Archdiocese of Philadelphia*.
    Philadelphia: Archdiocese of Philadelphia, 1976.

Cooke, Jacob E., ed. *The Federalist*. New York: World Publishing Co.,
    1961.

Coon, Jean. Brief for Appellant Levitt, *Cathedral Academy v. Committee
    for Public Education and Religious Liberty,* 413 U.S. 472 (1973).

Coons, John E. "Of Family Choice and 'Public' Education," *Phi Delta
    Kappan* 61 (September 1979):   10-13.

_____. *Private Wealth and Public Education*. Cambridge, Mass.: Belknap
    Press, 1970.

_____, and Sugarman, Stephen D. *Education by Choice: The Case for
    Family Control*. Los Angeles: University of California Press,
    1978.

Corwin, Edward S. *American Constitutional History*. New York: Harper
    Torchbooks, 1964.

_____. *The Constitution and What it Means Today*. Princeton: Princeton
    University Press, 1973.

_____. *A Constitution of Powers in a Secular State*. Charlottesville,
    Va.: The Michie Co., 1951.

_____. *Court over Constitution*. Gloucester, Mass.:   Peter Smith
    Publishers, 1957.

Creegan, Robert. "Subsidized Pluralism," *Schools and Society* 86 (Jan-
    uary 1958):   32-34.

Cunningham, Robert L. *Education: Free and Public*. Wichita: Center
    for Independent Education, n.d.

Cupps, Terry C. "Schools: Permissibility of Direct Governmental Aid to
    Sectarian Schools," *Washburn Law Journal* 20 (Fall 1980):   178-185.

"Current Comment," *America* 134 (13 March 1976):   193-194.

D'Alessio, Edward R. "Catholics Look to School Growth," *Sunday Star-Ledger,* 30 November 1980, p. 654.

The Debates and Proceedings in the Congress of the United States, Annals of the Congress of the United States, 1789-1824. Washington: 1834-1856.

Decreta Concilii Plenarii Baltimorensis Tertii. Baltimore: John Murphy and Co., 1886.

De Fiore, Leonard. Archdiocesan Schools Office, Washington, D.C. Interview, 22 January 1981.

"Diocese Schools Show Increased Enrollments," *The [Trenton] Monitor,* 3 November 1980, p. 18.

Doerr, Edd. *Parochiaid and the Law.* Silver Springs, Md.: Americans United for Separation of Church and State, 1975.

_____. *The Parochiaid Bomb.* Silver Springs, Md.: Americans United for Separation of Church and State, 1970.

Donohue, John W. "The Private School: An Island of Security?" *America* 144 (18 April 1981): 311-315.

Dougherty, John J., ed. *The Bishops of Newark: 1853-1978.* South Orange, N.J.: Seton Hall University Press, 1978.

Douglas, William O. *The Court Years: 1939-1975.* New York: Random House, 1980.

Doyle, Denis P. "Public Policy and Private Education," *Phi Delta Kappan* 62 (September 1980): 15-19.

Draney, T. P. *The American Proposition and Catholicism.* Albany: Catholic School Administrators Association of New York State, 1975.

_____. *The First Amendment and Freedom of Religion in Education.* Albany: Catholic School Administrators Association of New York State, 1975.

Drinan, Robert P. *Religion, the Courts and Public Policy.* New York: McGraw-Hill Book Co., 1963.

Drouin, Edmond G. *The School Question.* Washington: Catholic University of America Press, 1963.

Dubuque, Archdiocese of. *Catholic Schools Teachers Handbook,* 1977.

Duval, Benjamin S. "Constitutionality of State Aid to Nonpublic Elementary and Secondary Schools," *University of Illinois Law Forum,*
1970, p. 342.

"Education and Science," *The Kingdom of the Netherlands.* The Hague:
Government Printing Office, 1971, pp. 1-33.

Ehlers, Henry J., ed. *Crucial Issues in Education.* New York: Holt,
Rinehart and Winston, Inc., 1969.

Elam, Stanley M., ed. *A Decade of Gallup Polls of Attitudes toward
Education: 1969-1978.* Bloomington, Ind.: Phi Delta Kappa, Inc.,
1978.

_____. *The Gallup Polls of Attitudes toward Education: 1969-1973.*
Bloomington, Ind.: Phi Delta Kappa, Inc., 1973.

_____. "The Passing Parade," *Phi Delta Kappan* 62 (November 1980): 163.

Elford, George. *Trends in Education: Public and Private School Cooperation.* Columbus: University Council for Educational Administrators, 1976.

_____. "The Voucher Plan Debate," *America* 126 (29 January 1972):
87-91.

Emerson, Thomas I., et al. *Political and Civil Rights in the United
States.* Boston: Little, Brown and Co., 1967.

Encyclopedia Brittanica, 1972 ed. S. v. "Humanism."

English, Raymond. "For Tuition Tax Credits and Vouchers," *New York
Times.* 19 April 1981, p. E15.

Erickson, Donald. *The New "Public" Schools.* Wichita: Center for
Independent Education, 1977.

_____. *Public Controls for Nonpublic Schools.* Chicago: University of
Chicago Press, 1969.

_____. "Should *All* the Nation's Schools Compete for Clients and
Support?" *Phi Delta Kappan* 61 (September 1979): 14-17+.

Evenson, J. Eric. "State Regulation of Private Religious Schools in
North Carolina—A Model Approach," *Wake Forest Law Review* 16 (June
1980): 405-437.

Everson v. Board of Education, 330 U.S. 1 (1947).

Fellman, David. *Religion in American Public Law.* Boston: Boston University Press, 1965.

Fichter, Joseph H. *Parochial School: A Sociological Study.* Notre Dame: University of Notre Dame Press, 1958.

Fitzpatrick, Franklin E. "Supreme Court Vacancies and Catholic Schools," *The Tablet,* 30 September 1971, p. 1.

Flast v. Cohen, 392 U.S. 83 (1968).

Forster, Arnold, et al. Brief for the American Jewish Committee, et al. amici curiae, *Lemon v. Kurtzman,* 403 U.S. 602 (1971).

Fortkamp, Frank E. "Government Schools—A System in Trouble," *Inform 2* (November 1980): 1-4.

Fraenkel, Jack R. "Why a Comprehensive Program of Values Education Is Needed," *Social Education* 45 (February 1981): 101-107.

Freund, Paul A., et al. *Constitutional Law: Cases and Other Problems.* Boston: Little, Brown and Co., 1967.

_____, and Ulich, Robert. *Religion and the Schools.* Cambridge, Mass.: Harvard University Press, 1965.

Friedman, Daniel, et al. Brief for the Appellees, *Tilton v. Richardson,* 403 U.S. 672 (1971).

Friedman, David. *Toward a Competitive School System.* Wichita: Center for Independent Education, n.d.

Friedman, Milton. *Capitalism and Freedom.* Chicago: University of Chicago Press, 1972.

_____, and Friedman, Rose. *Free to Choose.* New York: Avon Books, 1981.

Frost v. Railroad Commission, 271 U.S. 583 (1926).

Gabel, Richard J. *Public Funds for Church and Private Schools.* Toledo: Murray and Heister, 1937.

Gaffney, Edward McGlynn. "Political Divisiveness along Religious Lines; The Entanglement of the Court in Sloppy History and Bad Public Policy," *St. Louis University Law Journal* 24 (September 1980): 205-236.

Gallup, George. "People Want Aid," *Freedom in Education* 23 (January/
    February 1981): 4.

_____. "Public Leans in Favor of 'Voucher Plan,'" 18 December 1980.

Gaustad, Edwin. *A Religious History of America*. New York: Harper and
    Row, 1974.

Germino, Dante. "Freedom and the Moral Order," *Communio* 7 (Fall 1980):
    243-258.

Giacoma, James M. "Committee for Public Education and Religious Liberty
    v. Regan: New Possibilities for State Aid to Private Schools," *St.
    Louis University Law Journal* 24 (September 1980): 401-424.

Gianella, Donald A. *"Lemon* and *Tilton:* The Bitter and the Sweet of
    Church-State Entanglement," *The Supreme Court Review,* 1971, pp.
    147-200.

Glazer, Nathan. "Ethnicity and Education: Some Hard Questions," *Phi
    Delta Kappan* 63 (January 1981): 386-389.

_____, and Moynihan, Daniel P. *Beyond the Melting Pot*. Cambridge,
    Mass.: MIT Press, 1970.

Gordis, Robert, et al. *Religion and the Schools*. New York: The Fund
    for the Republic, 1959.

Greeley, Andrew M. *The American Catholic: A Social Portrait*. New
    York: Basic Books, 1977.

_____. "Institutional Anti-Catholicism," *Advocate,* 25 (February 1981),
    p. 9.

_____. *Minority Students in Catholic Secondary Schools*. Unpublished
    manuscript (1981).

_____. *An Ugly Little Secret*. Kansas City: Sheed Andrews and McMeel,
    1977.

_____, et al. *Catholic Schools in a Declining Church*. Kansas City:
    Sheed and Ward, Inc., 1976.

_____, et al. *Young Catholics in the United States and Canada*. New
    York: Sadlier & Co., 1981.

Greene, Evarts B. *Religion and the State,* Ithaca, N.Y.: Cornell Uni-
    versity Press, 1959.

Guilday, Peter. *A History of the Councils of Baltimore*. New York: Arno Press and New York Times, 1969.

Hamilton, Alexander, et al. *The Federalist*. New York: Mentor Books, 1961.

Handbook for Private School Administrators. Prepared for U.S. Office of Education by the Council for American Private Education. Washington: Government Printing Office, 1974.

Handy, Robert T. "A Decisive Turn in the Civil Religion Debate," *Theology Today* 37 (October 1980): 342-350.

Harper v. Virginia State Board of Elections, 383 U.S. 663 (1966).

Hartnett, Robert C., ed. *The Right to Educate*. New York: America Press, 1949.

Hassard, John R. G. *Life of John Hughes*. New York: Arno Press and New York Times Press, 1969.

Higham, John. *Send These to Me*. New York: Atheneum Press, 1975.

Hitchcock, James. *On the Present Position of Catholics in America*. New York: National Committee of Catholic Laymen, 1978.

_____. "The Supreme Court and Religion: Historical Overview and Future Prognosis," *St. Louis University Law Journal* 24 (September 1980): 183-204.

Hooker, Clifford, ed. *The Courts and Education*. Chicago: University of Chicago Press, 1978.

Howe, Mark DeWolfe, ed. *Cases on Church and State in the United States*. Cambridge, Mass.: Harvard University Press, 1952.

_____. *The Garden and the Wilderness*. Chicago: University of Chicago Press, 1965.

Huck, Janet. "The Bells of St. Michael's," *Newsweek* 97 (20 April 1981): 67.

Humanist Manifesto I and II. Amherst, N.Y.: American Humanist Association, 1973.

Hunt v. McNair, 413 U.S. 734 (1973).

"Insight Time," *National Review* 33 (1 May 1981): 471.

Johannsen, Oscar B. *Private Schools for All*. Wichita: Center for
    Independent Education, 1976.

John Paul II, Pope. "The Church Wants to Communicate Christ to You,"
    USA: The Message of Justice, Peace and Love. Boston: St. Paul
    Editions, 1979, pp. 90-93.

_____. "Freedom of Conscience and of Religion," *l'Osservatore Romano*,
    19 January 1981, pp. 12-14.

_____. "Man's Entire Humanity Is Expressed in Culture," *France: Message
    of Peace, Trust, Love and Faith*. Boston: St. Paul Editions, 1980,
    pp. 184-210.

_____. "Pope's Message on Catholic Education," *l'Osservatore Romano*,
    30 April 1979, p. 4.

Johnson, Alvin W., and Yost, Frank H. *Separation of Church and State*.
    Minneapolis: University of Minnesota Press, 1948.

Kancelbaum, Joshua, et al. Brief for the Appellants in *Wolman v. Walter*,
    433 U.S. 229 (1977).

Katz, Wilber G. *Religion and American Constitutions*. Evanston, Ill.:
    Northwestern University Press, 1963.

Kaufman, Irving R. "Congress v. the Court," *New York Times Magazine*, 20
    September 1981, pp. 44+.

Kauper, Paul G. *Civil Liberties and the Constitution*. Ann Arbor: Uni-
    versity of Michigan Press, 1966.

_____. *Religion and the Constitution*. Baton Rouge: Louisiana State
    University Press, 1964.

_____. "The Walz Decision: More on the Religion Clauses of the First
    Amendment," *Michigan Law Review* 69 (December 1970):   179-210.

Kelly, Alfred H., and Harbison, Winfred. *The American Constitution:
    Its Origin and Development*. New York: W. W. Norton and Co., 1970.

Kelly, George A. *The Battle for the American Church*. New York: Double-
    day, 1979.

_____, ed. *Government Aid to Nonpublic Schools: Yes or No?* New York:
    St. John's University Press, 1972.

Kienel, Paul A. *The Christian School.* Wheaton, Ill.: Victor Books, 1974.

Kilpatrick, James J. "Conservatism at the High Court," *National Review* 33 (7 August 1981): 893-895.

Kirk, Russell. "Why Bother?" *National Review* 28 (21 December 1979): 1628.

Kizer, George. "An Analysis of the Drive for Public Funds for Parochial Schools: 1945-1963." Ph.D. dissertation, University of Oklahoma, 1964.

Kommers, Donald P., and Wahoske, Michael J. *Freedom and Education: "Pierce v. Society of Sisters" Reconsidered.* Notre Dame: Notre Dame Law School Press, 1972.

Krasicky, Eugene. "Ride in the Back of the Bus," *Catholic Mind* 74 (April 1976): 34-43.

Krauschaar, Otto F. *American Nonpublic Schools.* Baltimore: Johns Hopkins University Press, 1972.

_____. *Private Schools: From the Puritans to the Present.* Bloomington, Ind.: Phi Delta Kappa, 1976.

Kurland, Philip B. *Religion and the Law.* Chicago: Aldine Publishing Co., 1962.

LaFarge, Oliver. *We Need Private Schools.* Wichita: Center for Independent Education, 1954.

Lannie, Vincent P. *Public Money and Parochial Education.* Cleveland: Press of Case Western Reserve University, 1968.

LaNoue, George R., ed. *Education Vouchers: Concepts and Controversies.* New York: Teachers College Press, 1972.

Larson, Martin A. *When Parochial Schools Close.* New York: Robert B. Luce, Inc., 1972.

Lawler, Thomas B. *Standard History of America.* New York: Ginn & Co., 1937.

Lemon v. Kurtzman, 403 U.S. 602 (1971).

Lemon v. Kurtzman ("Lemon II"), 411 U.S. 192 (1973).

"A Lesson from Australia," *America* 144 (18 April 1981):   309-310.

Levin, Henry M. *The Failure of the Public Schools and the Free Market Remedy.* Wichita: Center for Independent Education, n.d.

Levitt v. Committee for Public Education and Religious Liberty, 413 U.S. 472 (1973).

Lewin, Nathan and Rapps, Dennis. Brief for Appellee Yeshiva Rambam, *Committee for Public Education and Religious Liberty v. Regan,* 444 U.S. 646 (1980).

Littell, Franklin H. *From State Church to Pluralism.* Garden City, N.Y.: Doubleday, 1962.

Love, Orlan. "Freedom of Choice for Inner-City Parents," Supplement to the *Catholic League Newsletter,* September 1980.

Lowell, C. Stanley. *The Church-State Fraud.* New York: Robert B. Luce, Inc., 1973.

Lynn, Robert W. "The Eclipse of a Public: Protestant Reflections on Religion and Public Education, 1940-1968." In *Theology and Church in Times of Change,* edited by Edward Long and Robert Handy. Philadelphia: Westminster Press, 1970.

McCarthy, Martha M. "Church and State: Separation or Accommodation?" *Harvard Educational Review* 51 (August 1981): 373-394.

McCluskey, Neil G. "Public Funds for Parochial Schools? Yes!" *Teacher's College Record,* October 1960, pp. 49-56.

McCollum v. Board of Education, 333 U.S. 203 (1948).

McDonald, Donald. *Religion and Freedom.* New York: The Fund for the Republic, 1958.

McGarry, Daniel D., and Ward, Leo. *Educational Freedom and the Case for Government Aid to Students in Independent Schools.* Milwaukee: Bruce Publishing Co., 1966.

McGrath, John J., ed. *Church and State in American Law.* Milwaukee: Bruce Publishing Co., 1962.

McLaughlin, Sr. Mary Raymond. *The Liberty of Choice: Freedom and Justice in Education.* Collegeville, Minn.: The Liturgical Press, 1979.

Malbin, Michael J. *Religion and Politics: The Intentions of the Authors of the First Amendment.* Washington: American Enterprise Institute for Public Policy Research, 1978.

Malone, Dumas. *Jefferson and His Time: The Sage of Monticello.* Boston: Little, Brown & Co., 1981.

Maritain, Jacques. *The Rights of Man and Natural Law.* New York: Charles Scribner's Sons, 1947.

Marnell, William H. *The First Amendment.* Garden City, N.Y.: Double-day, 1966.

Marty, Martin E. *The Public Church.* New York: Crossroad, 1981.

Massachusetts v. Mellon, 262 U.S. 447 (1923).

Mead, Sidney E. *The Lively Experiment.* New York: Harper and Row, 1963.

Medklenburger, James A., ed. *Education Vouchers: From Theory to Alum Rock.* Homewood, Ill.: ETC Publications, 1972.

Meek v. Pittenger, 421 U.S. 349 (1975).

Meiklejohn, Alexander. "Educational Cooperation between Church and State," *Law and Contemporary Problems,* Winter 1949, pp. 61-72.

Melvin, Edward J. *A Nation Built on God.* Huntington, Ind.: Our Sunday Visitor Press, 1975.

"H. L. Mencken Looks at Public Education," *Inform* 3 (March 1981): 1-4. (Reprint of a 1933 article)

Menendez, Albert J. "An Interview with Glen L. Archer," *Church and State* 29 (February 1976): 13-16.

Meyers, John F. Personal letter. Washington: 20 December 1979.

Mill, John Stuart. *On Liberty.* New York: Henry Holt and Co., 1898.

Miller, William L., et al. *Religion and the Free Society.* New York: The Fund for the Republic, 1958.

Minneapolis-St. Paul, Archdiocese of. *Administrators Handbook,* 1977.

Morgan, Richard E. *The Supreme Court and Religion.* New York: The Free Press, 1972.

Moynihan, Daniel P. New York, Interview, 4 October 1980.

_____. "Remarks upon Receiving the First Catholic League Award." New York, 4 October 1980.

_____. "Statement Prepared for Presentation to the Subcommittee on Education, Arts, and Humanities, Committee on Labor and Human Resources," U.S. Senate, 23 October 1979.

_____. "What Do You Do When the Supreme Court Is Wrong?" *The Public Interest* 57 (Fall 1979): 3–24.

_____. "Why Private Schools Merit Public Aid," *Independent School* 37 (May 1978): 18–21.

Munroe, David. *The Organization and Administration of Education in Canada.* Ottawa: Information Canada, 1974.

Murdock v. Commonwealth of Pennsylvania, 319 U.S. 105 (1943).

Murray, J. C. "Law or Prepossessions?" *Law and Contemporary Problems,* Winter 1949, pp. 23–43.

_____. *We Hold These Truths.* New York: Sheed and Ward, 1960.

Myers, Gustavus. *History of Bigotry in the United States.* New York: Capricorn Books, 1960.

Nagel, Robert F. "A Plague of Judges," *The Human Life Review* 7 (Winter 1981): 110–115.

National Catholic Welfare Conference. "The Constitutionality of the Inclusion of Church-Related Schools in Federal Aid to Education," *Georgetown Law Review* 50 (Winter 1961): 397–455.

National Conference of Catholic Bishops. *To Teach as Jesus Did.* Washington: United States Catholic Conference, 1972.

National Labor Relations v. Catholic Bishop of Chicago, 440 U.S. 490 (1979).

Nault, Richard L. "Institutional Jeopardy and Government Funding of Catholic Schools," *Momentum* 12 (February 1981): 39–41.

Neusner, Jacob. "How Should Jews Vote?" *National Review* 32 (17 October 1980): 1250–1252.

New Jersey, State of. "Transportation of Children Remote from School." N.J.R.S. Cum. Supp., Tit. 18, c. 14, § 8.

New York, State of. "Apportionment of State Monies to Nonpublic Schools." N.Y. Laws 1974, ch. 507, as amended by ch. 508.

_____. "Health and Safety Grants for Nonpublic School Children." N.Y. Laws 1972, c. 414 § 1, amending N.Y. Educ. Law, Art. 12, §§ 549-553 (Supp. 1972-1973).

_____. "Power to Designate Textbooks; Purchase and Loan of Textbooks; Purchase of Supplies." New York Sess. Laws 1965, c. 320, § 1.

New York, Archdiocese of. *Administrative Manual,* 1980.

Nolan, Richard. Brief for Appellee Schools, *Committee for Public Education and Religious Liberty v. Regan,* 444 U.S. 646 (1980).

"No Law but Our Own Prepossessions," *American Bar Association Journal,* June 1948, pp. 482-485.

Norwood v. Harrison, 413 U.S. 455 (1973).

Nowak, John E., et al. "Freedom of Religion," *Constitutional Law.* St. Paul: West Publishing Co., 1978, pp. 848-894.

Oaks, Dallin H., ed. *The Wall between Church and State.* Chicago: University of Chicago Press, 1963.

O'Brien, J. Stephen, and Vacca, Richard S. *The Supreme Court and the Religion-Education Controversy: A Tightrope to Entanglement.* Durham: Moore Publishing Co., 1974.

O'Brien, Timothy, and Zewe, Donald. "Hope in the Inner City," *Momentum* 12 (February 1981): 11-13.

Ohio, State of. "Distribution of Payments for Special Programs." Ohio Rev. Code Ann. § 3317.06 (Supp. 1976).

O'Neill, J. M. *Religion and Education under the Constitution.* New York: Harper and Brothers, 1949.

O'Reilly, James T. "The Memorare and the Constitution," *America* 144 (31 January 1981): 80-83.

O'Toole, Thomas J., ed. *Institute of Church and State,* 2. Villanova, Pa.: Villanova University School of Law, 1959.

Padover, Saul K. *The Complete Jefferson*. New York: Duell, Sloan and Pearce, Inc., 1943.

_____. *A Jefferson Profile*. New York: John Day Co., 1956.

Palko v. State of Connecticut, 302 U.S. 319 (1937).

Parsons, Wilfrid. *The First Freedom*. New York: Declan X. McMullen Co., Inc., 1948.

Paterson, Diocese of. *Administrator's Manual*, 1977.

Paul VI, Pope. "Elizabeth Ann Seton," *The Pope Speaks* 20 (1975): 204-208.

_____. "Heritage of Freedom," *The Pope Speaks* 21 (1976): 239-246.

_____. "A Life of Love for Others," *The Pope Speaks* 22 (1977): 222-225.

Pearson, George H. *Another Look at Education Vouchers*. Wichita: Center for Independent Education, n.d.

Pennekamp v. Florida, 328 U.S. 331 (1946).

Pennsylvania, State of. "Auxiliary Services." Act 194, § 1(a), Pa. Stat. Ann., Tit. 24, § 9-972(a); Act 195, § 1(a), Pa. Stat. Ann., Tit. 24, § 9-972(a).

_____. "Nonpublic Elementary and Secondary Education Act," Pa. Laws, Tit. 24, § 5601, Repealed.

_____. "Parent Reimbursement Act for Nonpublic Education." Pa. Laws 1971, Act 92, Pa. Stat. Ann., Tit. 24, §§ 5701 et seq. (Supp. 1973-1974).

Pfeffer, Leo. Brief for the American Association of School Administrators, et al. as amici curiae, *Lemon v. Kurtzman*, 403 U.S. 602 (1971).

_____. Brief for the Appellants, *Committee for Public Education and Religious Liberty v. Nyquist*, 413 U.S. 756 (1973).

_____. Brief for the Appellants, *Committee for Public Education and Religious Liberty v. Regan*, 444 U.S. 646 (1980).

_____. Brief for the Appellees, *Cathedral Academy v. Committee for Public Education and Religious Liberty*, 413 U.S. 472 (1973).

Pfeffer, Leo. Brief for the Appellees, *Levitt v. Committee for Public Education and Religious Liberty,* 413 U.S. 472 (1973).

_____. Brief for Committee for Public Education and Religious Liberty as amici curiae, *Wolman v. Walter,* 433 U.S. 229 (1977).

_____. "The 'Catholic' Catholic Problem," *Commonweal* 102 (1 August 1975): 302–305.

_____. *Church, State and Freedom.* Boston: Beacon Press, 1967.

_____. *God, Caesar and the Constitution.* Boston: Beacon Press, 1975.

_____. "Issues That Divide: The Triumph of Secular Humanism," *Journal of Church and State* 19 (Spring 1977): 203–216.

_____. *Religious Freedom.* Skokie, Ill.: National Textbook Co., 1977.

_____. "The Supremacy of Free Exercise," *Georgetown Law Journal* 61 (May 1973): 1115–1142.

_____. "Unionization of Parochial School Teachers," *St. Louis University Law Journal* 24 (September 1980): 273–294.

_____, and Thorn, William. Oral arguments in behalf of the Appellants, *Meek v. Pittenger,* 421 U.S. 349 (1975).

Philadelphia, Archdiocese of. *Parish Elementary School Policies and Procedures,* 1975.

Pierce v. Society of Sisters, 268 U.S. 510 (1925).

Pius X, Pope. *Codex Iuris Canonici.* Westminster, Md: Newman Press, 1963.

Pius XI, Pope. *Christian Education of Youth.* Washington: National Catholic Welfare Conference, 1936.

Plude, Frances F. *What's Happening to Catholic Schools?* New York: William H. Sadlier, Inc., 1974.

Pollack, Marvin. Brief for the Appellants, *Board of Education v. Allen,* 392 U.S. 236 (1968).

"Pope: Schools Are Heart of Church," *Catholic Standard and Times,* 26 November 1981, p. 12.

Portland-in-Oregon, Archdiocese of. *Policies and Regulations: Handbook of Elementary Schools Archdiocese of Portland,* 1976.

Powell, James M. "Public Schools and the First Amendment," *America* 139 (1/8 July 1978): 6-9.

President's Panel on Nonpublic Education. *Nonpublic Education and the Common Good.* Washington: U.S. Government Printing Office, 1972.

Prince v. Commonwealth of Massachusetts, 321 U.S. 158 (1944).

"Proceedings and Debates of the 95th Congress," *Congressional Record* 124, 14/15 August 1978.

Providence, Diocese of. *Manual of Policies and Regulations for Elementary and Secondary Schools,* 1976.

Quick Bear v. Leupp, 219 U.S. 77 (1908).

Raabe, William. "Parochial Schools and the IRS: The Scope of Administrative Control," *Taxes* 58 (July 1980): 494-499.

Radloff, John. "Public School Transportation in the United States: The Legal Status of Transporting the Parochial Pupils and of the Utilization of Transportation to Achieve Racial Balance." Ph.D. dissertation, University of Denver, 1969.

Ravitch, Diane. *The Great School Wars--New York City, 1805-1973.* New York: Basic Books, 1974.

_____. "The Way to Make Public Schools Good," *Washington Post,* 19 April 1981, p. C7.

Rector of Holy Trinity v. United States, 413 U.S. 457 (1892).

Reed, Fred. "The Color of Education," *Harper's* 262 (February 1981): 26-29.

Regan, Richard J. *American Pluralism and the Catholic Conscience.* New York: Macmillan and Co., 1963.

_____. *Private Conscience and Public Law.* New York: Fordham University Press, 1972.

_____. "Supreme Court Roundup: 1979 Term," *Thought* 55 (December 1980): 487-502.

Reilly, Robert T. "Good Luck, Father," *America* 145 (3 October 1981): 179-181.

Religion and the Schools: From Prayer to Public Aid. Washington: National Schools Public Relations Association, 1970.

Reutter, E. *Schools and the Law.* Dobbs Ferry, N.Y.: Oceana Publications, Inc., 1970.

_____, and Hamilton, Robert R. *The Law of Public Education* (with 1973 Supplement). Mineola, N.Y.: The Foundation Press, 1976.

Rhode Island, State of. "Legislative Findings—Declaration of Policy," General Laws of Rhode Island, § 16-51-1, Repealed.

Roemer v. Board of Public Works, 426 U.S. 736 (1976).

Ryn, Claes G. "The Things of Caesar: Notes toward the Delimitation of Politics," *Thought* 55 (December 1980): 439-460.

Sacred Congregation for Catholic Education. *The Catholic School.* Washington: United States Catholic Conference, 1977.

Sacred Congregation for the Causes of Saints. *Decree of Canonization of Blessed John Nepomucene Neumann.* Rome, 13 November 1976.

Savage, David G. "Expect a Battle over Tuition Tax Credits," *Phi Delta Kappan* 63 (February 1981): 411-412.

"School Prayer Draws Criticism from Harvard Professor," *Phi Delta Kappan* 62 (April 1981): 548.

Scribner, Jay D., ed. *The Politics of Education,* 76th Yearbook of the National Society for the Study of Education, Part II. Chicago: University of Chicago Press, 1977.

Seymour, Whitney. Brief for the American Civil Liberties Union as amici curiae, *Everson v. Board of Education,* 330 U.S. 1 (1947).

Shanker, Albert. "Tax Credits: The Myth of Parental Choice," *New York Times,* 25 January 1981, p. E9.

Shaughnessy, Gerald. *Has the Immigrant Kept the Faith?* New York: Macmillan Co., 1925.

Shaw, Richard. *Dagger John: The Life of Archbishop John Hughes.* New York: Paulist Press, 1977.

Shaw, Russell.   "Arguments, Attitudes and 'Aid'," *Momentum* 6 (December
    1975):   34-37.

_____. "A New Church-State Clash in the Offing?"   *Columbia* 61 (April
    1981):   33.

Sherbert v. Verner, 374 U.S. 398 (1963).

Sizer, Theodore R.   "Education and Assimilation: A Fresh Plan for
    Pluralism," *Phi Delta Kappan* 58 (September 1976):   31-35.

Sloan v. Lemon, 413 U.S. 825 (1973).

Smith, Edward Conrad, ed.   *The Constitution of the United States.*   San
    Francisco: Barnes and Noble Books, 1972.

Smith, Elwyn A.   *Religious Liberty in the United States.*   Philadelphia:
    Fortress Press, 1972.

Smith, Michael R., and Bryson, Joseph E.   *Church-State Relations: The
    Legality of Using Public Funds for Religious Schools.*   National
    Organization on Legal Problems of Education, 1972.

Sobran, Joseph.   "The Abortion Culture," *Human Life Review* 7 (Spring
    1981):   7-19.

_____. "Ethnicity or Faith," *National Review* 33 (12 June 1981):   679-
    680.

Sowell, Thomas.   "Patterns of Black Excellence," Supplement to the *Cath-
    olic League Newsletter,* August 1976.

Sorauf, Frank J.   *The Wall of Separation.*   Princeton: Princeton Uni-
    versity Press, 1976.

Spurlock, Clark.   *Education and the Supreme Court.*   Urbana, N.Y.:
    University of Ithaca Press, 1955.

"The State and Sectarian Education," *NEA Research Bulletin,* February
    1946, pp. 5-44.

Stokes, Anson P., and Pfeffer, Leo.   *Church and State in the United
    States.*   New York: Harper and Row, 1964.

Stravinskas, Peter M. J.   *Catholic Education: A New Dawn?*   Canfield,
    Ohio: Alba Books, 1977.

Stravinskas, Peter M. J. "Parents and Schools: The Right to Choose," an address to the Paterson Diocesan Home-School Federation, 5 October 1980.

Sullivan, Daniel J. *Public Aid to Nonpublic Schools.* Lexington, Mass.: D. C. Heath and Co., 1947.

Sullivan, Thomas. Brief for the Respondents, *Wheeler v. Barrera,* 417 U.S. 402 (1974).

Sweeney, David F. *The Life of John Lancaster Spaulding,* New York: Herder & Herder, 1966.

Swomley, John M. "The Catholic League: Civil Rights or Sectarian Pressure," *Church and State* 33 (October 1980): 14-17.

_____. *Religion, the State and the Schools.* New York: Pegasus Press, 1968.

Taft, Adon. "Day Schools are Key to Survival, Rabbi Says," *Miami Herald,* 3 April 1981, p. 5E.

Tavel, David. *Church-State Issues in Education.* Bloomington: Ind: Phi Delta Kappa, 1979.

Taylor, Judith K. "Educational Vouchers: Addressing the Establishment Clause," *Pacific Law Journal* 11 (July 1980): 1061-1083.

Thiessen, Elmer J., and Wilson, L. J. Rcy. "Curriculum in the Church-State Controversy," *Inform* 3 (January 1981): 1-8.

Tiedt, Sidney W. *The Role of the Federal Government in Education.* New York: Oxford University Press, 1966.

Tilton v. Richardson, 403 U.S. 672 (1971).

Torcaso v. Watkins, 367 U.S. 488 (1961).

Tortora, Anthony. *"Ex Parte* McCardle," *National Review* 32 (19 September 1980): 1140+.

Trenton, Diocese of. *Handbook of Policies and Practices for Elementary and Secondary Schools,* 1978.

Tribe, Laurence H. "Rights of Religious Autonomy," *American Constitutional Law.* Mineola, N.Y.: The Foundation Press, 1978, pp. 812-885.

Truax v. Corrigan, 257 U.S. 312 (1921).

Tussman, Joseph. *The Supreme Court on Church and State.* New York: Oxford University Press, 1962.

United States Office of Education and the Council for Private Education, eds. *Private Schools and the States.* Washington: Council for Private Education, 1977.

Valente, William D. *Law in the Schools.* Columbus: Merrill Publishing Co., 1980.

_____. *Overview of Constitutional Developments Affecting Individual and Parental Liberty Interests in Elementary and Secondary Education.* Wichita: Center for Independent Education, 1978.

Vitullo-Martin, Thomas. *Catholic Inner-City Schools.* Washington United States Catholic Conference, 1979.

_____. New York. Interview, 18 November 1980.

Wagner, Richard E., ed. *Government Aid to Private Schools: Is It a Trojan Horse?* Wichita: Center for Independent Education, 1979.

Walinsky, Adam. "Aid to Parochial Schools," *New Republic* 166 (7 October 1972): 18-21.

Walz v. Tax Commission, 397 U.S. 664 (1970).

Ward, Leo R. *Federal Aid to Private Schools.* Westminster, Md.: Newman Press, 1964.

Warshaw, Thayer S. *Religion, Education, and the Supreme Court.* Nashville: Abington, 1979.

West, E. G. "Choice or Monopoly in Education," *Inform* 3 (March 1981): 4-9.

_____. *Nonpublic School Aid.* Toronto: Lexington Books, 1977.

Wheeler v. Barrera, 417 U.S. 402 (1974).

Whelan, Charles M. "The School Aid Decisions: 'Not Dead but Sleeping'," *America* 131 (7 July 1973): 6-8.

Whitehead, John W. *The Separation Illusion.* Milford, Mich.: Mott Media, 1977.

Williams, Dennis A., et al. "The Bright Flight," *Newsweek* 97 (20 April 1981): 66-73.

_____. "Why Public Schools Fail," *Newsweek* 97 (20 April 1981): 62-65.

Wills, Garry. *Explaining America: The Federalist.* Garden City, N.Y.: Doubleday & Co., 1981.

Wilson, Ellen. *Catholic Education: A Backward Look at the Future.* New York: National Committee of Catholic Laymen, 1979.

Wilson, John F. *Church and State in American History.* Englewood, N.J.: D.C. Heath and Co., 1965.

Wisconsin v. Yoder, 406 U.S. 205 (1972).

Wolman v. Walter, 433 U.S. 229 (1977).

Woodward, Bob, and Armstrong, Scott. *The Brethren.* New York: Avon Books, 1981.

"Yeast for the Schools," *America* 143 (4 October 1980): 182.

Young, David. Brief for the Appellees, *Wolman v. Walter,* 433 U.S. 229 (1977).

_____. "Implementation of Wolman," *Proceedings . . . Fourteenth National Meeting of Diocesan Attorneys.* Washington: United States Catholic Conference, April 1978, pp. 215-243.

Yudof, Mark. "Law-and-Education Research: Past and Future," *New York University Education Quarterly* 11 (Fall 1979): 10-15.

Zion, Sidney. "A Decade of Constitutional Revision," *New York Times Magazine,* 11 November 1979, p. 26, and 18 November 1979, p. 76.

Zirkel, Perry A., ed. *A Digest of Supreme Court Decisions Affecting Education.* Bloomington, Ind.: Phi Delta Kappa, 1978.

Zorach v. Clauson, 343 U.S. 306 (1952).